The United States OBLITERATE THE LEADERSHIP GAP! Collection

by Eric Z

Text © 2017 Eric Z.of www.TheKidsBooks.Blogspot.com

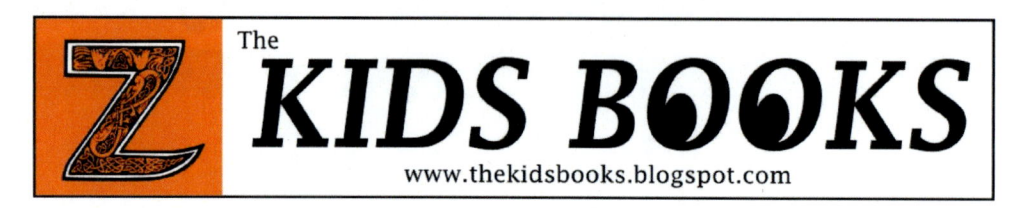

The Z KIDS BOOKS
www.thekidsbooks.blogspot.com

All rights reserved

All images CC-BY-2.0 and CC-BY-3.0:

This file is a work of a sailor or employee of the U.S. Navy, taken or made as part of that person's official duties. As a work of the U.S. federal government, the image is in the public domain.

This file has been identified as being free of known restrictions under copyright law, including all related and neighboring rights.

Except for Sammy the Seal who is exclusively owned and cared for by ©Eric Z:

That's me!

Did you miss the new coloring books?

Get a free sample!

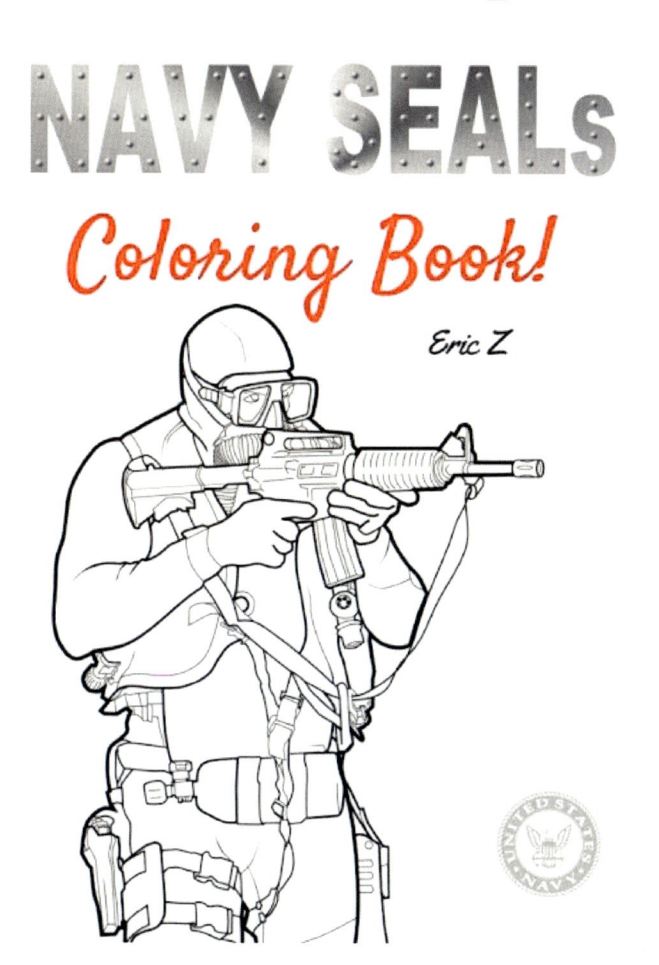

NAVY SEALs Coloring Book!

Eric Z

Type this in any browser and get your FREE sample:

bit.ly/sealcolor

Table of Contents

Navy SEALs for Kids - Book 1:
S.E.A.L. = SEa, Air, Land — 8
BUD/S = Basic Underwater Demolition/SEAL Training. — 16
Phase 1: Physical Conditioning (7 weeks) — 17
HELL WEEK! — 17
Phase 2: Combat Diving (7 weeks): — 21
Phase 3: Land Warfare (7 weeks) — 33
Parachute Jump School (3 weeks) — 34
SEAL Qualification Training (SQT) (26 weeks) — 35
Advanced Weapons Training: — 37
DEMOLITIONS: — 39
The SEAL Teams — 43

Navy SEALs for Kids - Book 2 - Weapons:
Sidearms: Pistols + Daggers — 51
    Sig Sauer P226 — 51
    HK 45C — 54
    KA-BAR Knife — 55
Rifles — 56
    M4A1 — 56
    MK13 CQBR — 58
    HK 416 — 59
    FN SCAR L/H — 60
    Barrett M82 Anti-Material Rifle — 63
    MK 11 SR25 (M110) — 65
    MK12 SPR — 66
    MK14 EBR — 67
    MK15 MacMillan TAC-50 — 67
Submachine guns — 68
    HK MP5 — 69
    HK MP7 — 72
Machine guns — 75
    M240 Machine Gun — 76

MK 46 (M249) Light Machine Gun	77
MK 48 Machine Gun	79
M134 Minigun	80

Recoilless rifles and Grenade Launchers — 82
- Carl Gustaf Recoilless Rifle — 82
- AT4 — 85
- M203 Grenade Launcher — 88
- M32 Grenade Launcher — 90

Equipment and other Good Stuff — 91
- Laser Target Designators — 91
- Nightvision — 92

Animals — 96
- DOLPHINS — 96
- SEA LIONS — 99

TOP SECRET: CLASSIFIED! — 103

Navy SEALs for Kids - Book 3 - H.A.L.O.
Briefing — 113
- Your mission: — 113
- The surroundings: — 113
- INSERTION: — 114
- EXTRACT: — 114
- Equipment: — 115

The Mission Begins — 118
- Insertion — 118
- Target — 126
- Extraction — 130

Bonus Section — 138
- The U.S. Navy Parachute Team, The Leap Frogs! — 138

Your adventure continues here! — 145

Navy SEALs
For Kids
by Eric Z

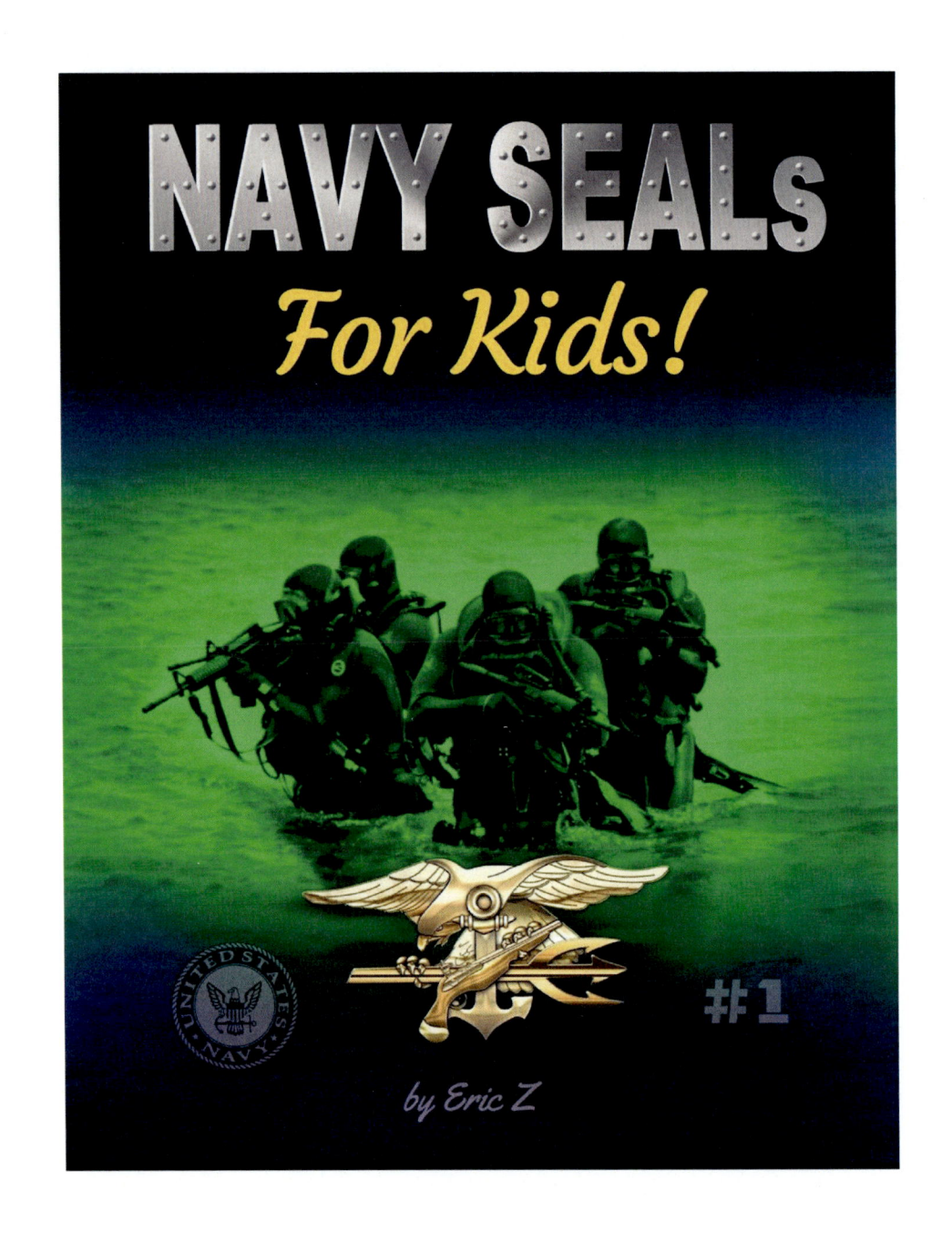

To all the kids who want to be a NAVY SEAL

If you persist, you will succeed!

S.E.A.L. = SEa, Air, Land

There are some things you should know before you try out for the Navy SEALs.

The Navy SEALs don't take just anyone, you must pass a tough physical test to be accepted to Navy SEALs training.

Assignment to BUD/S is conditional on passing the SEAL Physical Screening Test (PST).

For the physical program, you must:
1. Swim five hundred yards in less than nine minutes.
2. Do eighty to one-hundred push-ups in two minutes.
3. Do eighty to one-hundred sit-ups in two minutes.
4. Fifteen to twenty pull-ups.
5. Run one and a half miles in nine minutes — in boots!
6. See Stew Smith's page for more info:
    http://www.stewsmith.com/linkpages/NavySEALprep.html

Can you do 100 push ups?

Yes, he said ONE HUNDRED PUSH UPS!

100 PUSH-UPS in 2 minutes:

You can do it!

100 SIT-UPS in 2 minutes:

You gotta be fit to be a SEAL!

US NAVY

20 PULL-Ups:

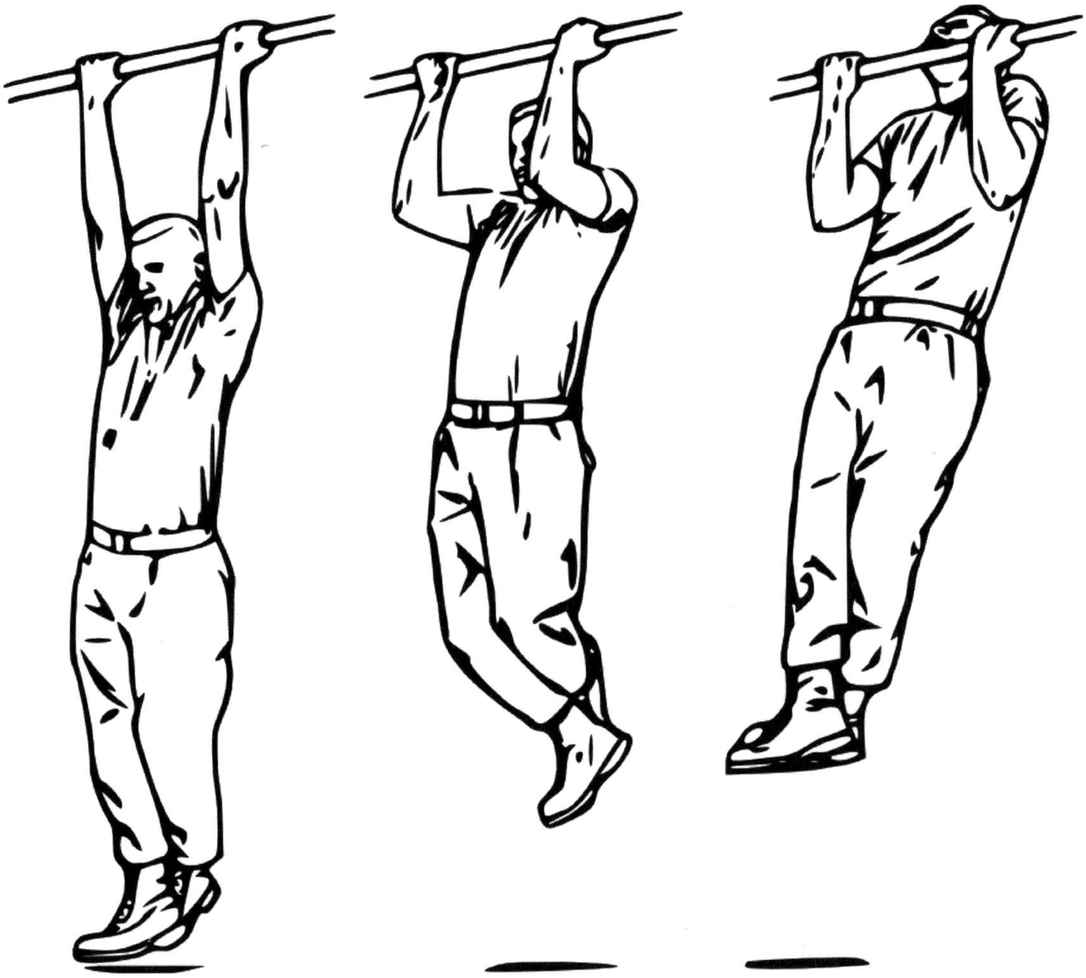

Swim 500 yards in 9 minutes:

With the Combat Swimmer Sidestroke

Run one and a half miles in 9 minutes...

...in boots and full gear!

Heckler & Koch 416

If you pass the physical test and get accepted to the Navy SEAL school, you will then go to the next phase of SEAL training - BUD/S.

BUD/S = Basic Underwater Demolition/SEAL Training.

Those unable to pass the final test are removed from the SEAL
training pipeline and reclassified into other jobs in the Navy.

FN SCAR assault rifle

Phase 1: Physical Conditioning (7 weeks)

The first phase of BUD/S assesses SEAL candidates in physical conditioning, water competency, teamwork and mental tenacity. Physical conditioning utilizes running, swimming and calisthenics
and grows harder and harder as the weeks progress. Candidates will participate in weekly four mile timed runs in boots and timed obstacle courses, swim distances up to two miles wearing fins in the ocean and learn small boat seamanship.

HELL WEEK!

The first two weeks of basic conditioning prepare candidates for the third week, also known as "Hell Week." During Hell Week, candidates participate in five and a half days of continuous training,
each candidate sleeps at most four hours during the entire week and runs more than 200 miles and does physical training for more than
20 hours per day.

This is the hardest part!

Did you get that?! 20 hours in the water:

And the mud:

And the water again:

And the sand, all while you do grueling tasks:

**If you survive Hell week ... you made it!
Now you go on to Combat Diving training.**

Phase 2: Combat Diving (7 weeks):

In phase 2 you will learn how to swim and breathe underwater with different SCUBA devices. Besides that your trainers will test you — underwater! This is another very difficult part of SEAL training. Overcoming your fear of the water, and performing at the same time will push you to your limits; physically and mentally — many candidates do not make it past this phase!

An instructor monitors a candidate's use of his scuba gear

Navy SEAL candidates must learn to survive in the water with their hands and feet tied together!

A Navy SEAL enters a mini-submarine

Navy SEALs emerging from the water. More often, a beach landing would take place at night — under the cover of darkness.

We usually do this at night.

US NAVY

A Navy SEAL practicing diving from a boat — at high speed!

Easy Peasy!

A SEAL emerging from the kelp with his Heckler & Koch MK23 pistol.

Before they were called Navy SEALs, they were called "Frogmen".

The early frogmen pioneered combat swimming, closed-circuit diving, underwater demolitions (UDT), and midget submarine (dry and wet submersible) operations. They were the first Navy SEALs.

In 1983, they were officially renamed from UDT to Navy SEALs.

The UDT's patch

Navy SEALs are deployed by aircraft carriers:

I love the food on this boat!

US NAVY

27

And boats:

And submarines:

And mini-submarines:

And even Osprey's!

Phase 3: Land Warfare (7 weeks)

Here you will learn basic weapons, demolitions, land navigation, patrolling, rappelling, marksmanship and small-unit tactics.

US Navy Mark 12 special purpose rifle

Parachute Jump School (3 weeks)

After the land warfare phase you go on to learn skydiving! But this isn't any ordinary skydiving. In parachute jump school you will learn to land in hostile territory — at night! Also HALO training, that is <u>H</u>igh <u>A</u>ltitude <u>L</u>ow <u>O</u>pening... so you can surprise the enemy!

SEAL Qualification Training (SQT) (26 weeks)

After parachute jump school comes SEAL Qualification training, here you will learn:
- Advanced weapons training
- Small unit tactics
- Land navigation
- Demolitions
- Cold weather training in Kodiak, Alaska
- Medical skills
- Maritime operations
- Survival, Evasion, Resistance and Escape training

Maritime Operations Training:

This is my favorite part

US NAVY

Advanced Weapons Training:

Carl Gustav recoilless rifle

Navy SEALs firing the Carl Gustav recoilless rifle

Students at SQT conduct a room clearing exercise:

Heckler & Koch MP5

DEMOLITIONS:

Finally ... you get to blow stuff up!

No... THIS is my favorite part!!!

And finally the last phase of SQT - Cold weather training:

YES! Navy SEALS must learn how to ski and shoot at the same time!

I love sliding on my belly...

US NAVY

Graduation from SQT culminates in the awarding of the coveted Navy SEAL Trident – after which new SEALs immediately are assigned to a SEAL Team and begin advanced training for their first deployment.

It was tough but I finally graduated!

The Navy SEALs Trident:

Only Navy SEALs are allowed to wear this!

The SEAL Teams

SEAL Team 1

SEAL Team 2

SEAL Team 3

SEAL Team 4

SEAL Team 5

United States Naval Special Warfare Development Group, formerly known as SEAL team 6:

SEAL Team 7

SEAL Team 8

SEAL Team 10

The End

NAVY SEALS
For Kids
WEAPONS

by Eric Z

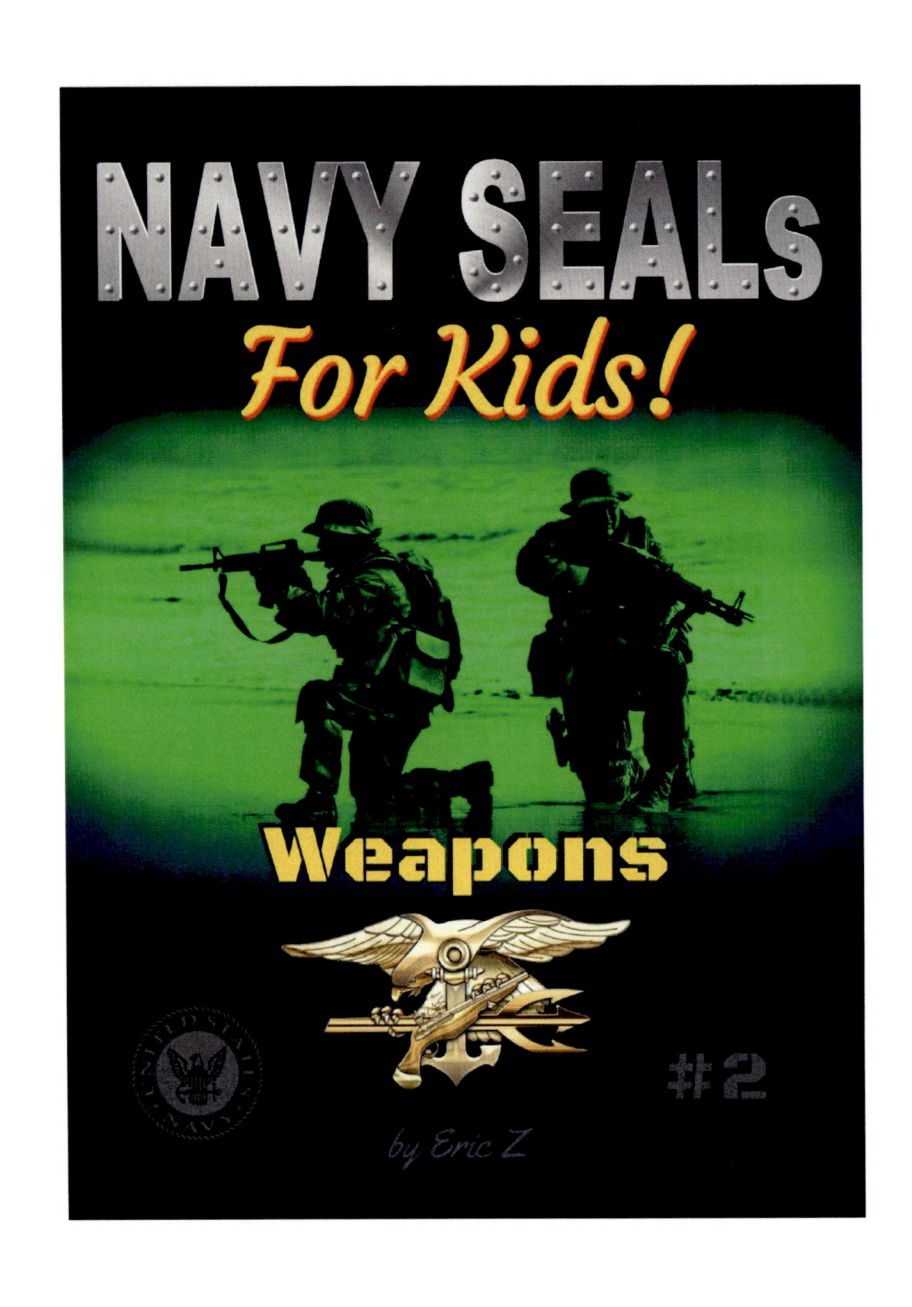

Before you start your adventure, we must WEAPONIZE you.

As a Navy SEAL you must become an expert with your weapons.

Read on and get to know your new daily tools, and some surprising ones near the end of the book!

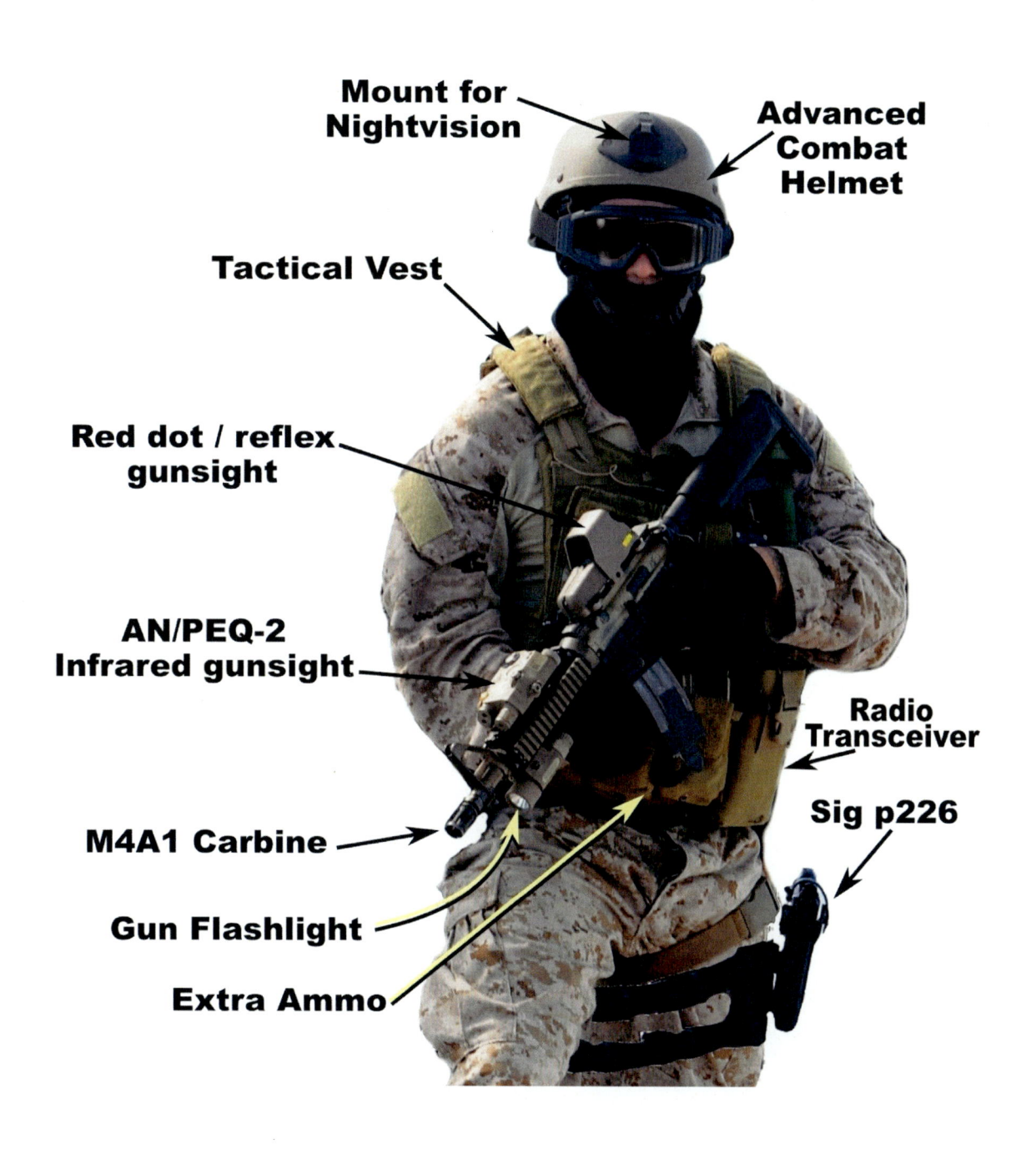

- Mount for Nightvision
- Advanced Combat Helmet
- Tactical Vest
- Red dot / reflex gunsight
- AN/PEQ-2 Infrared gunsight
- Radio Transceiver
- Sig p226
- M4A1 Carbine
- Gun Flashlight
- Extra Ammo

Sidearms: Pistols + Daggers

Sig Sauer P226

Calibre: 9mm
Magazine Capacity: 10 rounds

Pistols and knives are also called "side arms".

A Navy SEAL with the M4A1 carbine rifle and his Sig p226 side arm.

A Navy SEAL emerges from the water with his Sig 226:

I can hold my breath
for 20 minutes!

HK 45C

Calibre: .45 ACP
Magazine Capacity: 10 rounds

The Heckler and Koch 45C is more powerful than the Sig 226 and has more capabilities:

You can put a SILENCER on the threaded barrel, and there is a rail under the barrel; you can put a laser or flashlight on it for night time!

KA-BAR Knife

The United States Marines Ka-Bar knife is also a side arm the Navy SEALs use:

Who needs a knife? When you have TEETH!

US NAVY

Rifles

M4A1

The M4A1: Calibre 5.56 x 49 mm, is very versatile and is based on the M-16 Assault Rifle, the standard rifle of the US armed forces.

You can mix and match the M4A1 almost anyway you want, you can even put a GRENADE LAUNCHER on it...

The M4A1 with a grenade launcher mounted under the barrel:

Firing the M4A1:

MK13 CQBR

"CQBR" means Close Quarters Battle Rifle.

When engaging enemy forces inside buildings, you want a smaller, lighter, more maneuverable rifle.

The MK13 CQBR is based on the M4A1 rifle. It has a shorter barrel and a lighter RECEIVER — the top part of the rifle.

HK 416

The HK416 is also 5.56 x 49mm calibre, just like the M4A1. The HK also has long rails on top of and below the barrel:

This makes it real easy to customize with scopes, laser targeters, or even a bipod; like in the picture below:

FN SCAR L/H

The FN SCAR is a MODULAR assault rifle.

"Modular" means you can change the parts really quickly.

There are two versions of the FN SCAR:

1. The big version "H" in 7.62 mm NATO calibre

2. The smaller version "L" in 5.56 mm NATO calibre

All you have to do is just change the barrels and you have a different rifle!

Navy SEAL with an FN SCAR L (Light):

ELCAN C79 Telescopic sight:

Navy SEAL with an FN SCAR H (Heavy):

Barrett M82 Anti-Material Rifle

The Barrett M82 is so BIG — it is called an "anti-material" rifle; because you can use it against cars and tanks! Well, maybe not a Main Battle Tank, but a smaller tank for sure:

The Barrett M82 shoots a .50 calibre "BMG" bullet — it's HUGE!

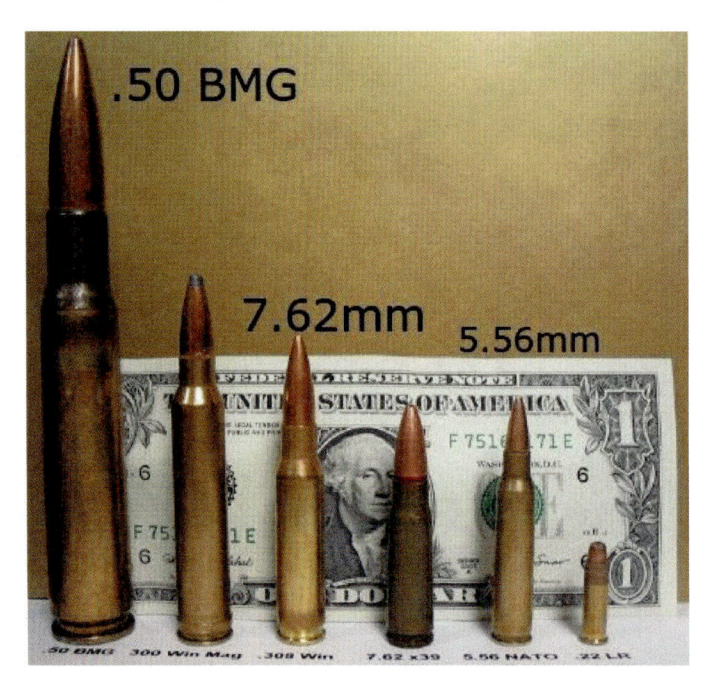

The .50 calibre BMG (Browning Machine Gun) bullet goes much farther than smaller bullets. This is why it is a favorite calibre for SNIPERS.

- Muzzle Velocity   2,800 fps (853 mps)
- Muzzle Energy 11,500 foot-pounds (15,582 J)
- Maximum Range   7,450 yd (6,812 m)
- Maximum Effective Range   2,000 yd (1,829 m)

MK 11 SR25 (M110)

The MK 11 is a 7.62 x 51 mm calibre SNIPER rifle.

MK12 SPR

The MK 12 "SPR" or Special Purpose Rifle, shoots the 5.56mm calibre bullet, and is also primarily used as a sniper rifle.

MK14 EBR

EBR= Enhanced Battle Rifle

The MK14 EBR is a 7.62 x 51mm calibre highly customizable rifle. It is based on the older M-14 rifle:

MK15 MacMillan TAC-50

The TAC-50 is another sniper rifle which shoots the huge .50 calibre bullet:

Submachine guns

A machine gun fires automatically, as many bullets as you want, with ONE pull of the trigger.

A "sub" machine gun does too, but it is called a submachine gun because it shoots a smaller pistol bullet, instead of a rifle bullet.

7.62mm - Rifles

5.56mm - Rifles

9mm - Pistols and Submachine guns

Rifle and Pistol Ammunition

HK MP5

The Heckler and Koch MP5 is one of the most popular submachine guns in the world. It shoots the 9mm bullet and can be mounted with scopes, silencers, and suppressors:

MP 5 with a suppressor and larger fore grip:

The rear sight of the HK MP5 is a DIOPTER sight, also called a "peep sight."

You aim the gun by "peeping" through the hole:

The MP5 holds 30 rounds (bullets) in its magazine. It is also really tough and can be used in the water, just right for Navy SEALs!

Trijicon ACOG — Advanced Combat Optical Gunsight:

HK MP7

The Heckler and Koch MP7 is a very small submachine gun which fires the high velocity 4.6 x 30mm bullet.

4.6 x 30mm cartridge. The brass case is 30mm long:

MP 7 fitted with a suppressor and red dot sight:

Aimpoint M68 CCO — Close Combat Optical Sight:

The compact size and power of the 4.6 mm calibre make it a super popular gun for the special forces of the world.

Romanian special forces firing the HK MP7:

AN/PEQ-2 Infrared Illuminator:

Machine guns

A machine gun is different than a rifle. Although they may fire the same bullets as a rifle, a machine gun is designed to fire A LOT of bullets continuously.

For this reason, machine guns are usually BELT FED. The bullets are not in a magazine, but on a belt, which is fed through the machine gun.

You can also change the barrel of a machine gun really fast, so you can fire all day!

Barrel change on an M240 machine gun:

M240 Machine Gun

Calibre: 7.62mm NATO

M240 mounted on a Humvee:

MK 46 (M249) Light Machine Gun

Calibre: 5.56mm NATO

The MK 46 Light Machine Gun is a super versatile machine gun that can be used as a SAW "Squad Automatic Weapon" or, with a scope mounted, even as a sniper rifle:

A U.S. Army Ranger with a MK 46 light machine gun providing overwatch in Iraq 2009; notice the M68 CCO red dot sight mounted on top. RED DOT sights can also be used on machine guns!

View through a red dot sight:

MK 48 Machine Gun

The Mark 48 machine gun is like the MK 46 but it fires the bigger 7.62 mm bullet.

Although the MK 48 is bigger than the MK 46, it is still light enough to fire standing up like a rifle:

M134 Minigun

Machine guns are a very important part of the armed forces, and probably the COOLEST of all the guns is the MINIGUN!

Calibre 7.62mm NATO

The minigun is an ELECTRIC six barreled ROTARY machine gun that fires 2,000 to 6,000 rounds per minute!

Miniguns are used by all of the United States armed forces, but the Navy SEALs use them on their SWCC — Special Warfare Combat Craft, otherwise known as ... BOATS!

Insignia of the SPECIAL BOAT TEAMS:

Recoilless rifles and Grenade Launchers

Carl Gustaf Recoilless Rifle

The Carl Gustaf is an 84mm "recoilless rifle" but it resembles a ROCKET LAUNCHER.

However the inside of the barrel does have grooves called "rifling" which make the munitions spin as they come out of the barrel. This stabilizes them during their flight to the target.

All rocket launchers and recoilless rifles have a huge back blast!

Inertia principle of the Recoilless Rifle:

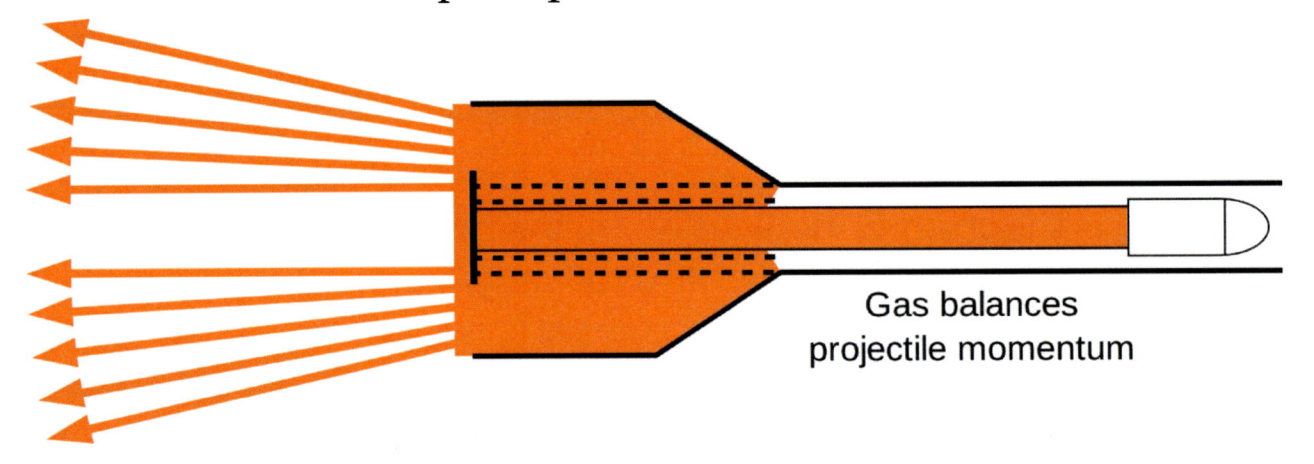

Gas balances projectile momentum

Special forces fire the Carl Gustaf in Basra Iraq. You can actually see the PROJECTILE leaving the barrel in this photo:

Just type this into any browser;

▶▶bit.ly/GustaF◀◀

... to see a **surprise** presentation about the Carl Gustaf Recoilless Rifle :-)

AT4

The AT4 is also an 84mm recoilless rifle, but it is DISPOSABLE. It is made to be fired just once; afterwards you discard the launcher tube:

The AT4 launcher tube and a cartridge with foldable fins.

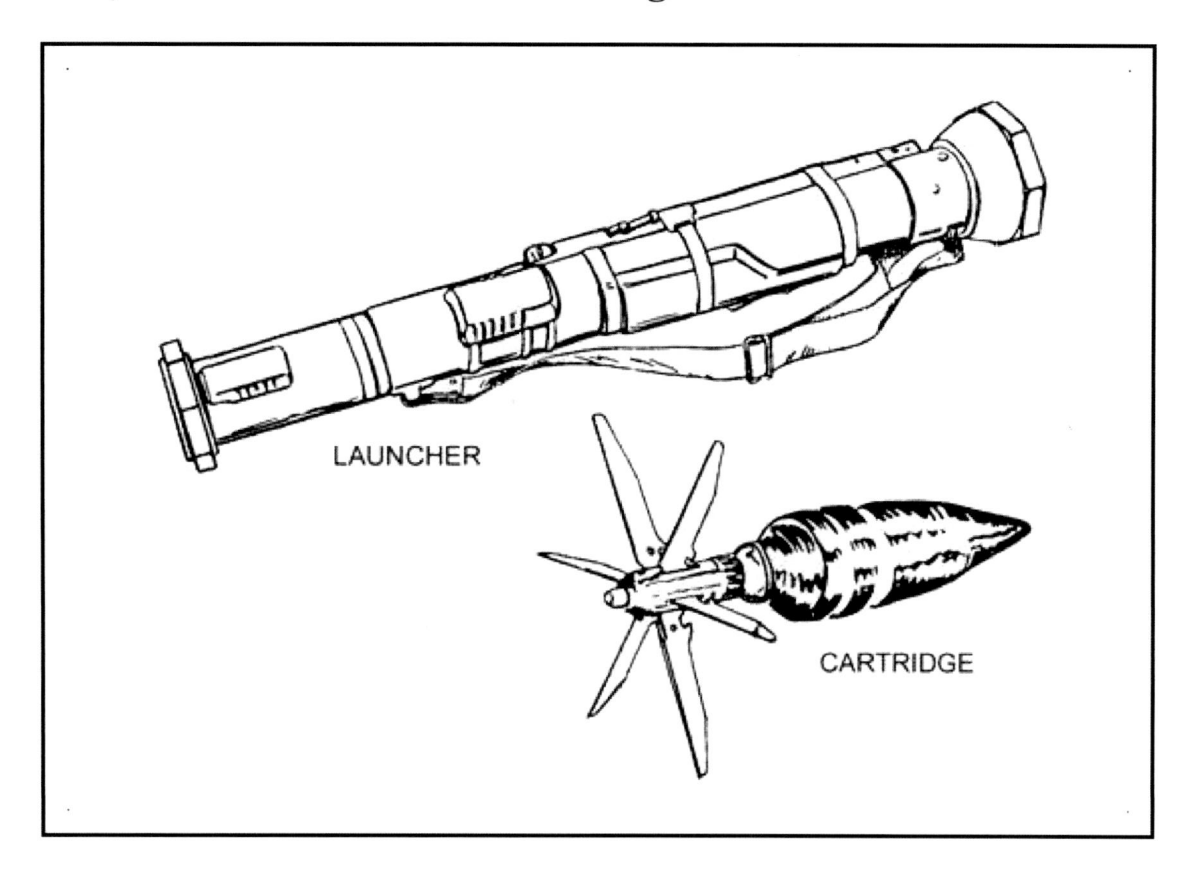

After firing and leaving the tube, the fins unfold to stabilize its flight. Unlike the Carl Gustaf, the AT4 has a smooth bore and does not have rifling to spin stabilize the projectile.

pro·jec·tile
/prəˈjektl,prəˈjekˌtīl/
noun: **projectile** plural noun: **projectiles**
A missile designed to be fired from a rocket or gun.
Synonyms: missile, rocket, bullets.

M79 Grenade Launcher

The M79 grenade launcher is a single shot gun that can lob a 40mm grenade over 350 meters!

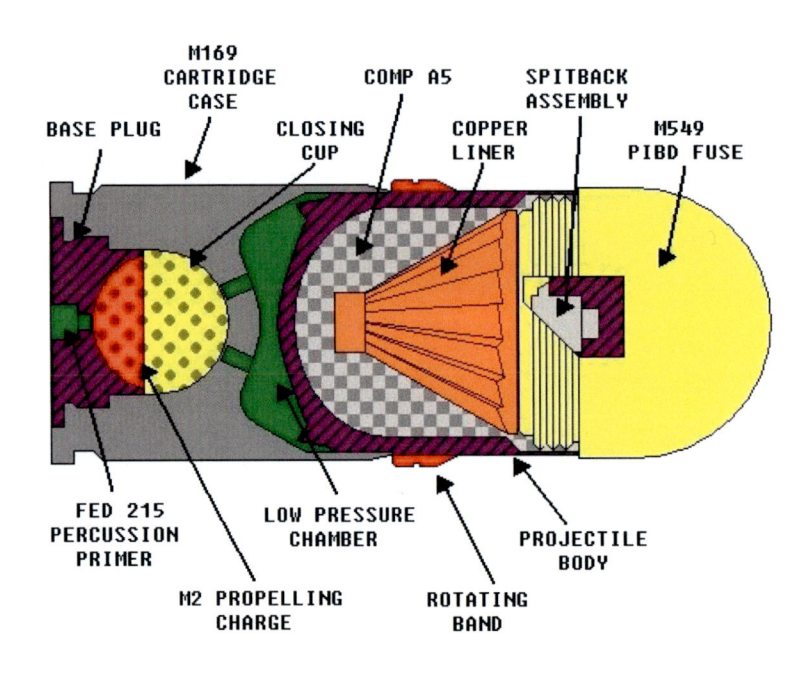

Cutaway view of a 40mm high-explosive grenade

M203 Grenade Launcher

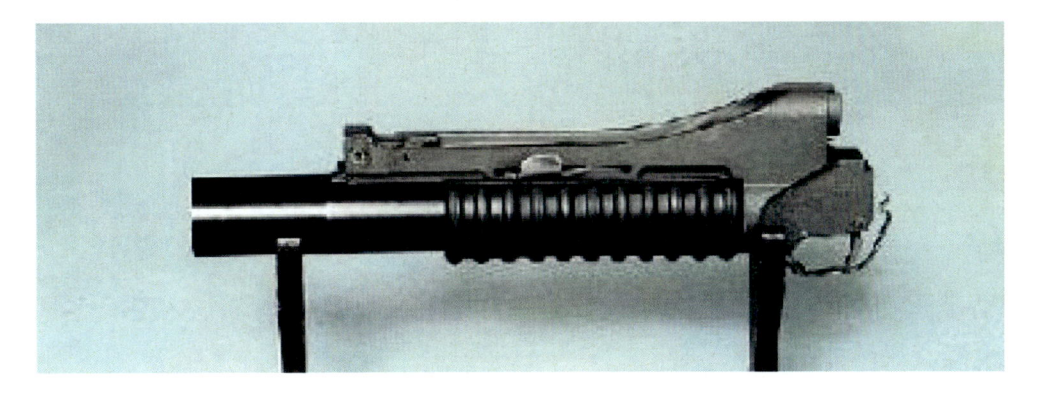

The M203 grenade launcher fits underneath almost any rifle:

M-16 with M203 Grenade Launcher

M4 Rifle with M203 Grenade Launcher

The M203 fires the exact same shells as the M79 and has the same range and accuracy. It is gradually replacing the M79 — why carry two weapons when you can carry one?

Because of the grenade's LOW VELOCITY, the soldier must aim very high. This is like a HOWITZER cannon which lobs a shell up in the sky, so that it can come down on top of the target — instead of hitting its front side.

how·itz·er
/ˈhouətsər/
noun: **howitzer** plural noun: **howitzers**
A short gun or cannon for firing shells on high trajectories at low velocities.

M32 Grenade Launcher

The M32 Grenade Launcher is a "rapid fire" weapon and can shoot SIX 40 mm grenades in under THREE seconds!

That's a whole lot of FIREPOWER!

M32 Grenade Launcher with an M2A1 red dot sight:

Equipment and other Good Stuff

Laser Target Designators

Not all weapons shoot bullets or grenades.

Some "shoot" laser light!

The Navy SEAL on the right is illuminating a target with the laser target designator, as his buddy on the left covers him.

You illuminate a target on the ground for an AIRSTRIKE.

Nightvision

Being able to see in the dark is one of the most important capabilities of the special forces.

PANORAMA night vision goggles:

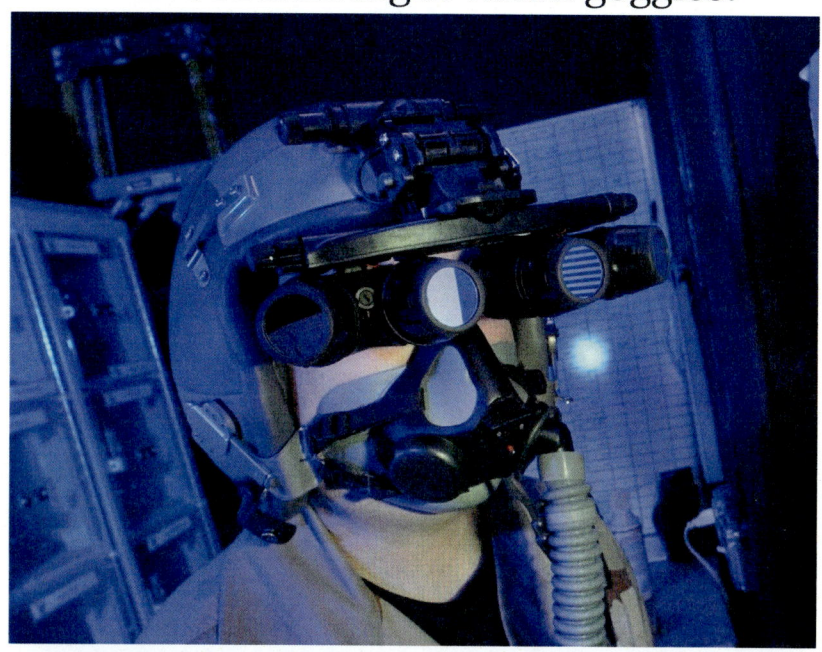

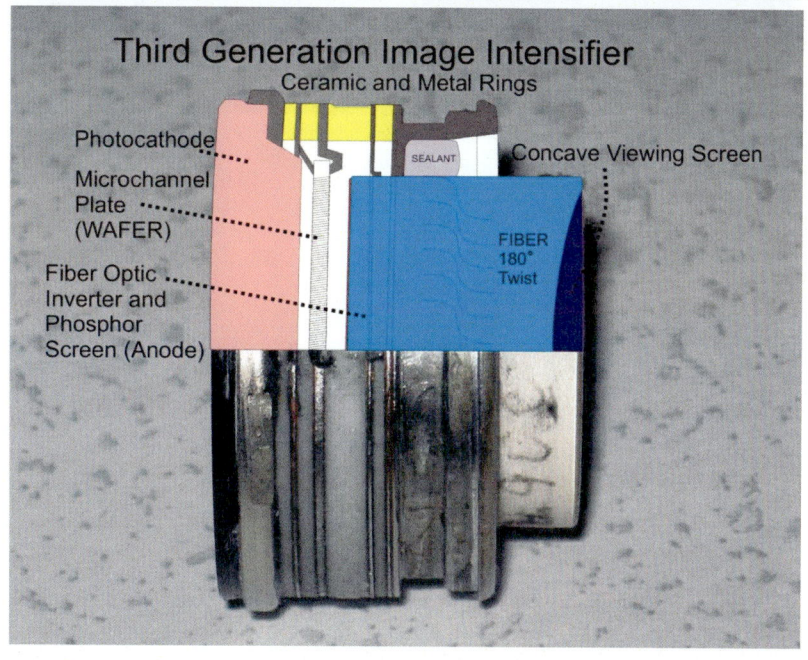

Night vision goggles use an IMAGE INTENSIFIER to amplify the light. Even in darkness there is a little light, especially on a moonlit night.

The image intensifier does this ELECTRONICALLY. For every PHOTON entering the tube, the intensifier will emit even more.

This way you can take the little bit of light available at night, MULTIPLY it, and see in the dark.

There is only one small disadvantage to night vision: it's ALL GREEN!

Photons (light!) go in, and MORE come out = night vision!

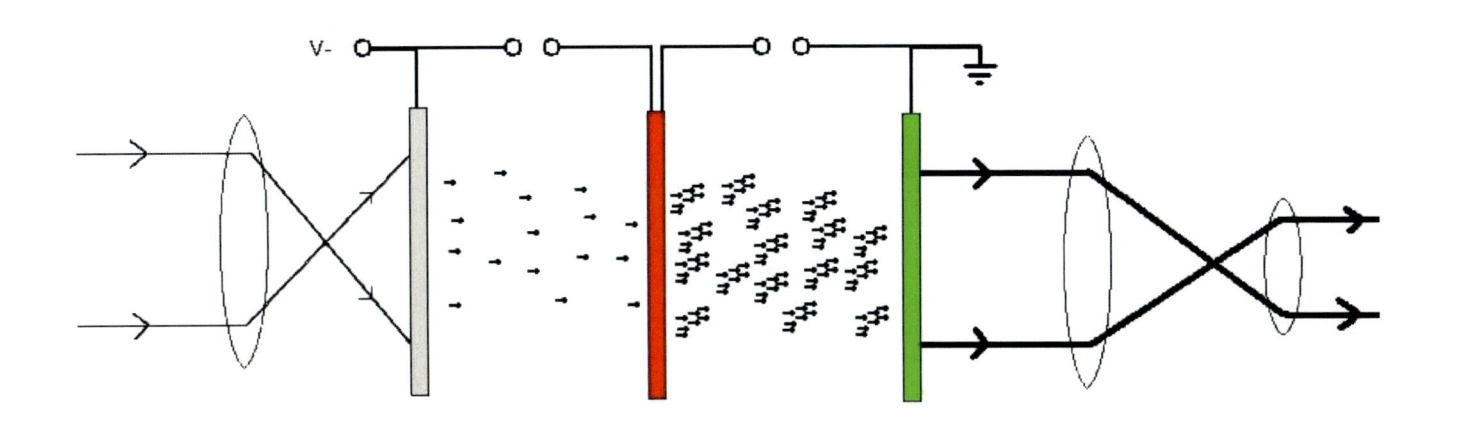

Hey! Everything's green!

Question: How do you aim your rifle when you are wearing night vision goggles?

Answer: With the INFRA-RED LASER mounted on your rifle!

When you are wearing night vision goggles, you cannot use the normal sight on your rifle.

Instead, you use the infra-red laser and point it at your target. Wherever the laser light dot appears, your bullet will hit!

Infra-red light is invisible to the naked eye, but your night vision goggles can see it.

But beware, sometimes the enemy has night vision goggles too, and can see your laser, and YOU!

Animals

"Weapons" aren't just knives, guns, grenades, bazookas, and machine-guns you know... animals can be WEAPONIZED too!

However, most animals are used only to help Navy SEALs find people — like enemy soldiers, and things — like bombs, and act as super sensitive eyes and ears for the soldier.

DOLPHINS

Dolphins have their own built in SONAR.

Sonar uses sound waves to detect objects.

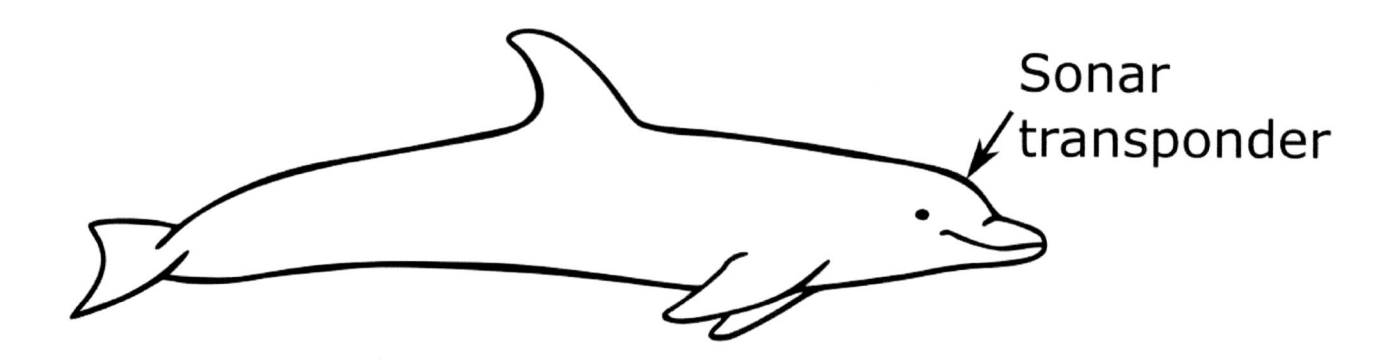

Sonar transponder

This is also called ECHO LOCATION.

The echo location of dolphins is BETTER than any man made device ever ... EVER!

This is why dolphins are probably the most valuable animal for the Navy because...

A dolphin can find an enemy anti-ship MINE, and report it to his Navy handlers BEFORE it blows up a ship and hurts anyone:

so·nar

/ˈsōˌnär/

noun: **sonar**

A system for the detection of objects under water and for measuring the water's depth by emitting sound pulses and detecting or measuring their return after being reflected.

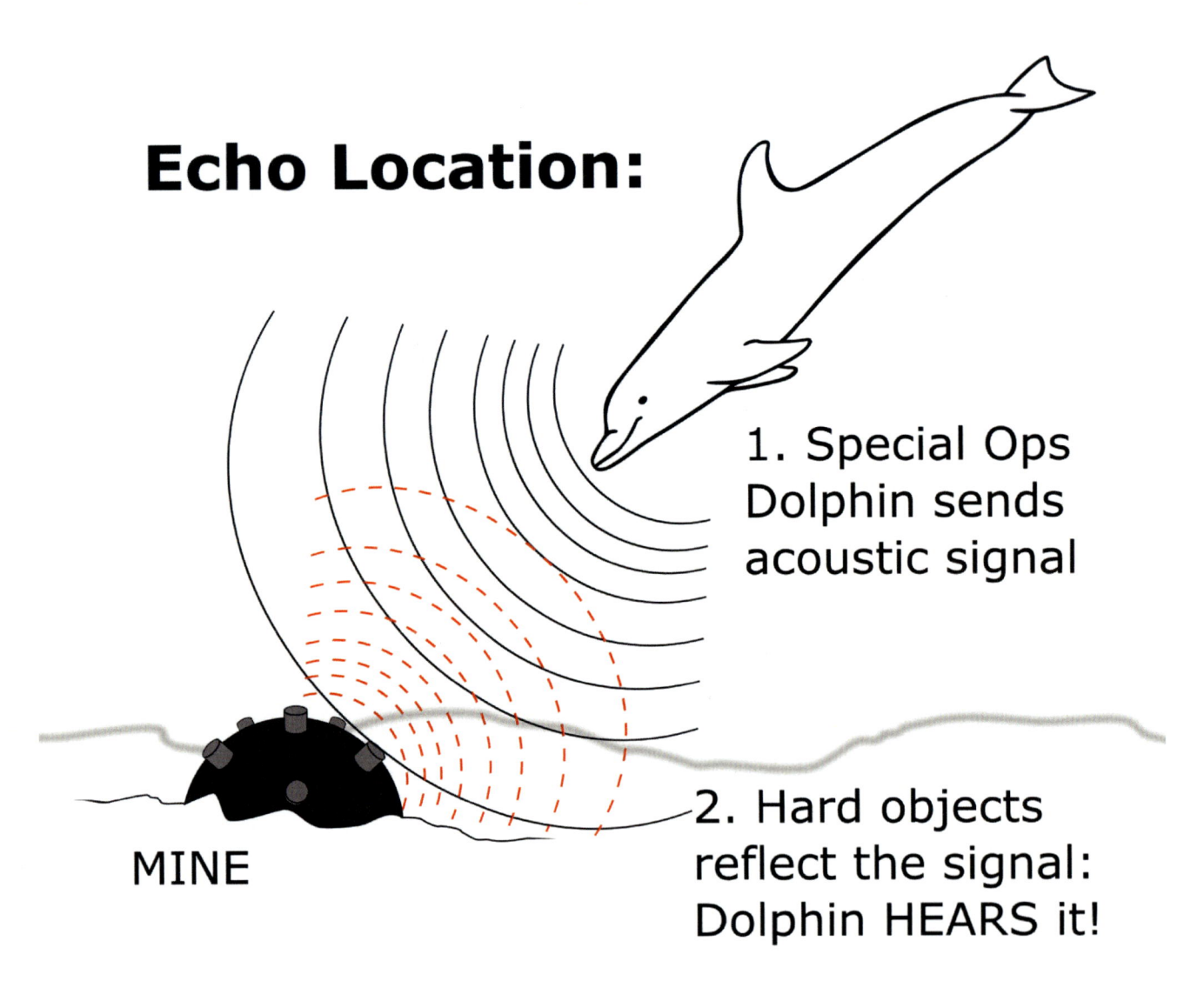

Echo Location:

1. Special Ops Dolphin sends acoustic signal

2. Hard objects reflect the signal: Dolphin HEARS it!

MINE

K-Dog, a bottlenose dolphin, leaps out of the water while training in the Persian Gulf. Attached to his fin is a "pinger" that allows his handler to keep track of him when he's out of sight.

SEA LIONS

The California Sea Lion

Zalophus californianus

Sea Lions are sometimes called seals, but there IS a difference...

...Seals don't have EARS!

No ears = Seal:

Don't worry, he can hear you!

With ears = Sea Lion!

These special forces Sea Lions and Dolphins are part of the NMMP: the Navy Marine Mammal Program based in San Diego California.

They are ready to go AROUND THE CLOCK, and have been used in the Vietnam War as well as the Iraq War!

Sea Lions are used to locate mines and bombs underwater. Once a Sea Lion does find one, he will then put a radio locator on it, so the Navy can find it and destroy it...

To see the videos just type this into any browser:

▶▶bit.ly/theNMMP◀◀

One of my proudest moments! US NAVY

TOP SECRET: CLASSIFIED!

The existence of the following programs can neither be confirmed nor denied:

If you can train an animal to find a mine, you can also train one to...

- PLANT a mine
- Attach bombs to ships...
- Attack enemy divers who are trying to bomb YOUR ship...
- Plant listening devices...

I am a DEADLY weapon

"Force protection"

The Navy uses dolphins and sea lions as SENTRIES to protect harbor installations and ships against unauthorized human swimmers ... BAD GUYS!

When an ENEMY DIVER is detected by a dolphin, the dolphin approaches from behind and bumps a device into the back of the enemy's air tank.

This device is attached to a buoy which then EXPLODES, alerting the Navy of the intruder.

Sea lions carry a similar device in their mouth, but instead attach it by hand-cuffing one of the enemy's limbs.

The animals depend on their superior underwater senses and swimming ability to defend against counterattacks.

A Sea Lion HANDCUFFING an enemy diver:

BOOM! GAME OVER for the enemy diver!

And that concludes this Navy SEALs adventure, *for now*...

The END

NAVY SEALS
For Kids
H.A.L.O.
by Eric Z

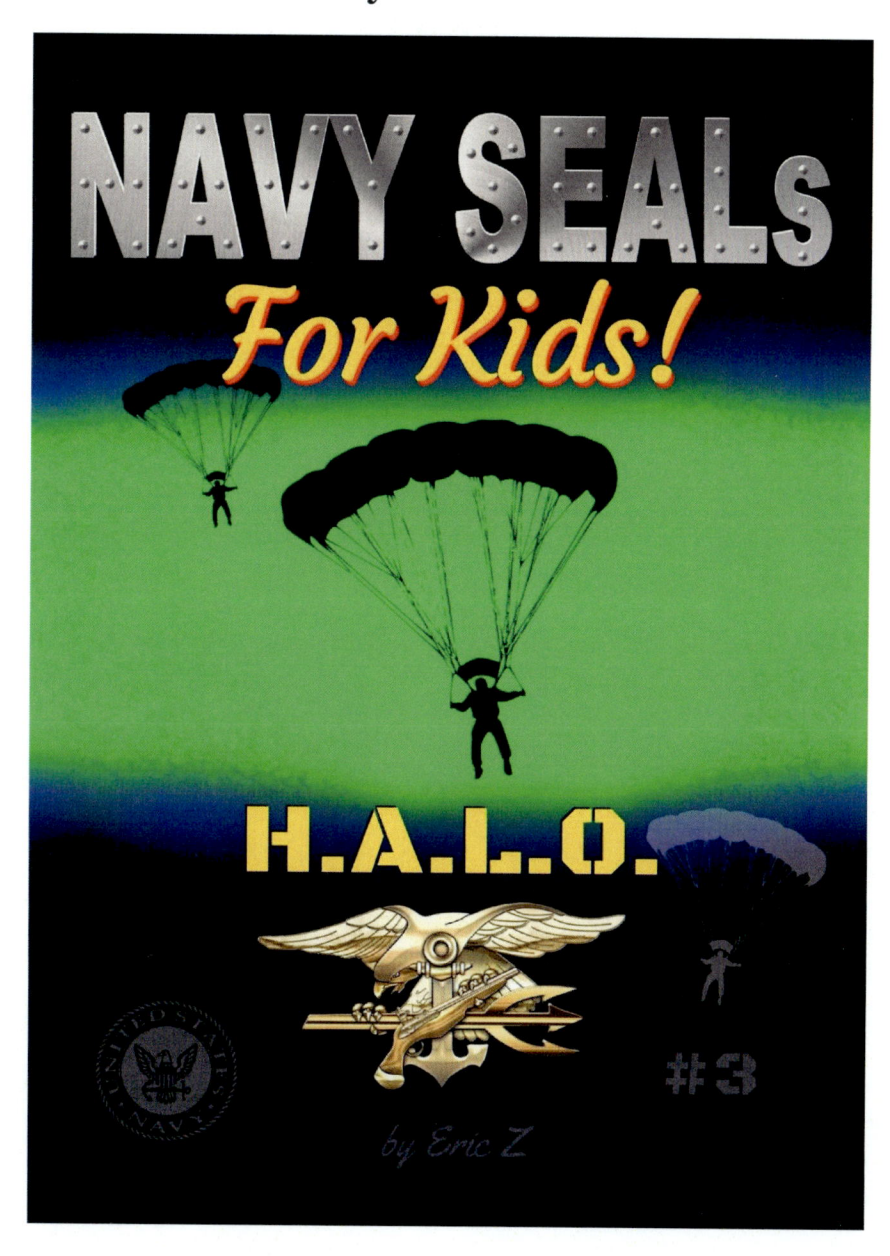

They're coming...

...thump thump thump thump thump thump thump thump thump thump thump thump thump thump thump thump thump thump thump **thump** **THUMP!**

NAVY

Here I come!

But you don't see them,

They come at night, under the cover of darkness...

And you don't hear them!

The Navy SEALs use a lot of TACTICS to approach the enemy and surprise him.

tac·tic

/ˈtaktik/

noun

plural noun: **tactics**

1. an action or strategy carefully planned to achieve a specific end.
2. *synonyms:* strategy, scheme, stratagem, plan, maneuver, method, expedient, gambit, move, approach, tack, device, trick, ploy, dodge, ruse, machination, contrivance, wangle, shift

One of the most effective tactics is called "HALO."

HALO means **H**igh **A**ltitude **L**ow **O**pening.

The Navy SEALs jump out of an aircraft at high altitude, but do not open their parachutes until they are very close to the ground. This enables them to avoid being seen by enemy RADAR.

However, this is also very dangerous, because they do not have a lot of time to open the emergency parachute if the main parachute does not work.

ra·dar
/ˈrāˌdär/
noun
noun: **radar**

1. a system for detecting the presence, direction, distance, and speed of aircraft, ships, and other objects, by sending out pulses of high-frequency electromagnetic waves that are reflected off the object back to the source.

Paragliding:

The Navy SEALs also don't have to jump out of the plane from right above the target.

Thanks to the High Glide Ratio Parachutes—HGRP's, the Navy SEALs can PARAGLIDE them up to 50 kilometers to the target.

That means the plane can fly from a safe distance outside the borders of enemy territory, as the SEALs parachute, and then glide IN to enemy territory!

par·a·glid·ing
/ˈperəˌglīdiNG/
noun
noun: **paragliding**

1. a sport in which a wide canopy resembling a parachute is attached to a person's body by a harness in order to allow them to glide through the air after jumping from or being lifted to a height.

Navy SEALs on an extended glide to the target landing zone.

I'm a STEALTH SEAL!

Briefing

We are starting at 04:00 hours!!!

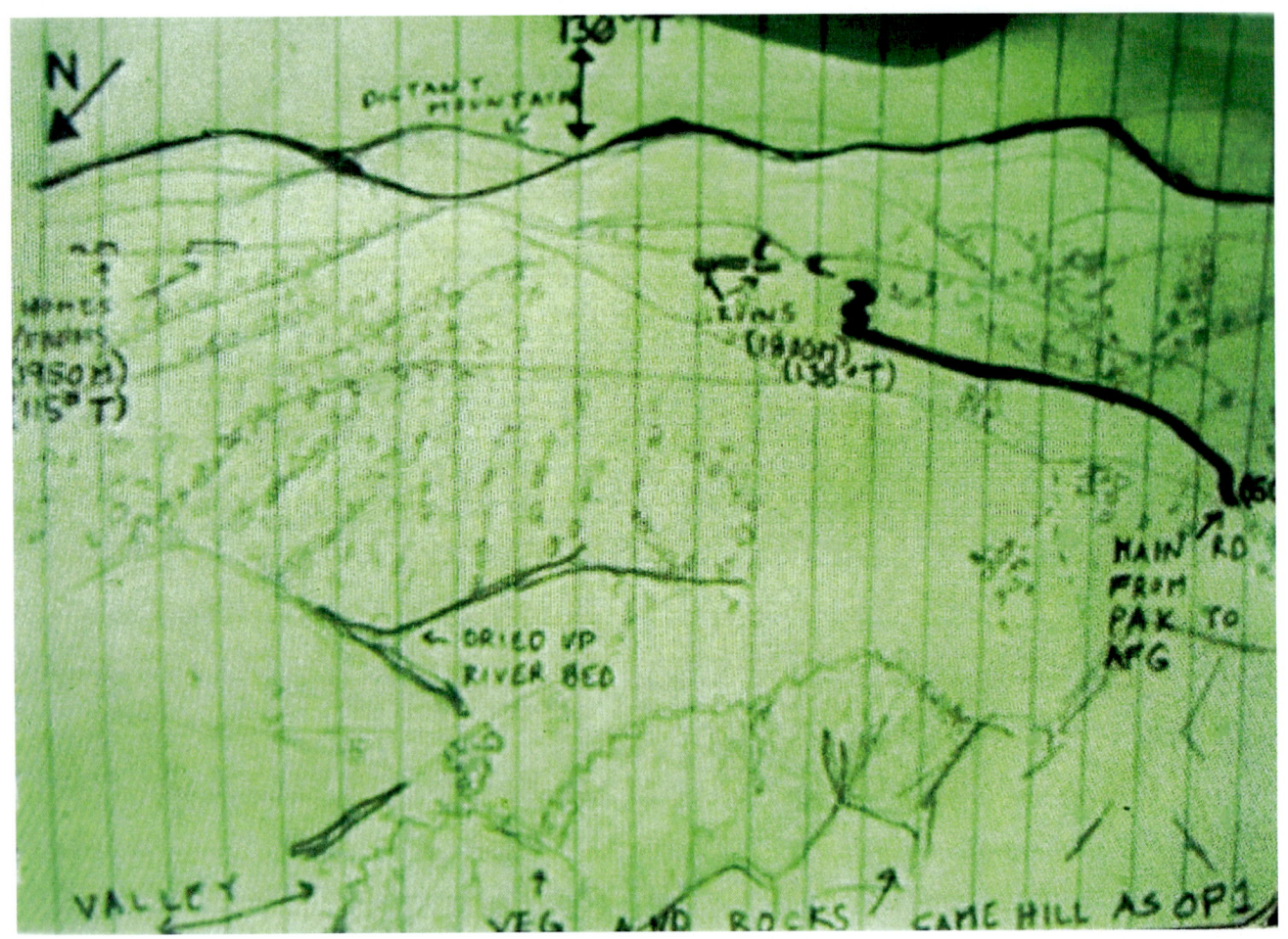

(Note: This is an actual map from an actual Navy SEALs mission.) [1]

Your mission:

To rescue a hostage, an American scientist, from the enemy stronghold.

The surroundings:

The enemy stronghold is deep in the jungle and near a river.

---

[1] Search "Operation Red Wings" in Google

INSERTION:

Insertion will be with a C-17 Globemaster III . You depart the aircraft at 04:00 hours under the cover of darkness.

You will HALO in, rendezvous at SECTOR X, then proceed to the target.

Once on target you will neutralize all enemy combatants, and rescue the hostage.

EXTRACT:

You will then proceed on foot to rendezvous point XX 5 kilometers downstream on the river to be picked up by your buddies in the SWCC.

SWCC — Special Boat Teams

Special Warfare Combatant-craft Crewmen

Equipment:

"FAST" Tactical Helmet

- Night Vision Mount
- Side Rail
- Battery Pack and Radio
- Microphone
- "Ears" Hearing Protection +Speaker

The "FAST" tactical helmet is lightweight and has a cut-out for the earphones. It also has side rails so you can mount all sorts of stuff on your helmet like flash lights, battery packs, and night vision.

Wait...does he have a beard?!

YES, special forces are just that: SPECIAL!

So they can have a beard when they are on field operations and need to blend in better.

Or, they just can't get to shaving because they are so busy fighting!

You will also see Navy SEALs quite often with plain old Skater helmets. They wear these helmets for H.A.L.O. missions and anytime they parachute.

The smooth helmet does not get caught in the lines of the parachute. This can happen really quickly when you are jumping out of an aircraft flying at 15,000 feet and 200+ miles per hour!

A Hand Altimeter is used to monitor your descent.

CRITICAL altitude is 3,500 feet where you MUST open your chute!

A hand altimeter worn by a Navy SEAL

A standard aircraft altimeter

The Mission Begins

Insertion

The team takes off at 04:00 hours as planned in the C-17 Globemaster III.

They climb to 25,000 feet and fly to the jump zone...

C-17 General Characteristics:
Crew: 3 (2 pilots + 1 loadmaster or JUMPmaster)
Capacity: 102 paratroopers
Length: 174 ft (53 m)
Wingspan: 169.8 ft (51.75 m)
Height: 55.1 ft (16.8 m)
Cruise speed: Mach 0.74 (515 mph)
Range: 2,785 mi (4,482 km) ; 6,456 mi (10,390 km) with paratroopers
Service ceiling: 45,000 ft (13,716 m)
Landing distance: 3,500 ft (1,100 m)

The JUMPMASTER monitors the team and checks their gear.

For very high jumps, above 15,000 feet, there will also be a physical technician—the "PT"— to monitor their oxygen masks and make sure they are fit to jump. At high altitude you can get HYPOXIA and not even know it!

The Jumpmaster then controls exactly when they jump out of the aircraft, at the right altitude and correct coordinates, to ensure that they make it to the target.

When the time is right, he opens the rear ramp of the aircraft and gets the team ready for the jump; behind the lines and into enemy territory!

hy·pox·i·a
/hīˈpäksēə/
noun: hypoxia
A deficiency in the amount of oxygen reaching the tissues.

ARE YOU READY?!

GO!!!

Navy SEALs leave aircraft with oxygen mask and gear

Heavy equipment is dropped separately

If the team plans to land in water they wear fins...

119

The team "link up" during free fall...

Formation flight for descent

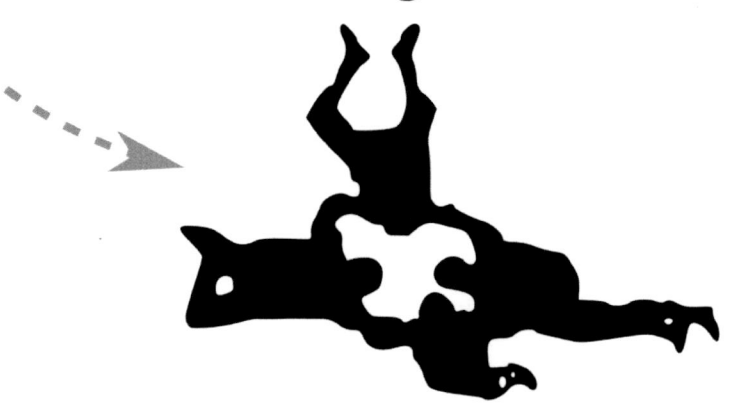

This way the team lands together on the same spot, and they can quickly gather their gear and proceed to the target!

Critical: monitor hand altimeter and open the chute at right time:
PULL THE RIPCORD!!!

DANGER ZONE!
If your chute does not open
You only have a split second
to open the *reserve* chute!

Navy SEALs fly into enemy territory - **UNseen and UNheard!**

SEALs land near designated **Rendesvous** point near TARGET...

SEALs collect equipment, and proceed to target and fulfill mission objectives: free hostage, capture bad-guy, **DESTROY TARGET!**

The SEALs glide into sector X as planned...

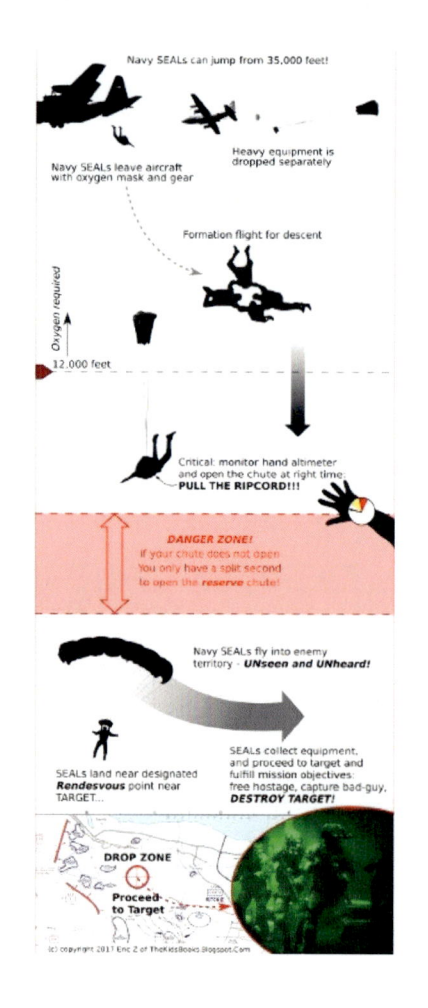

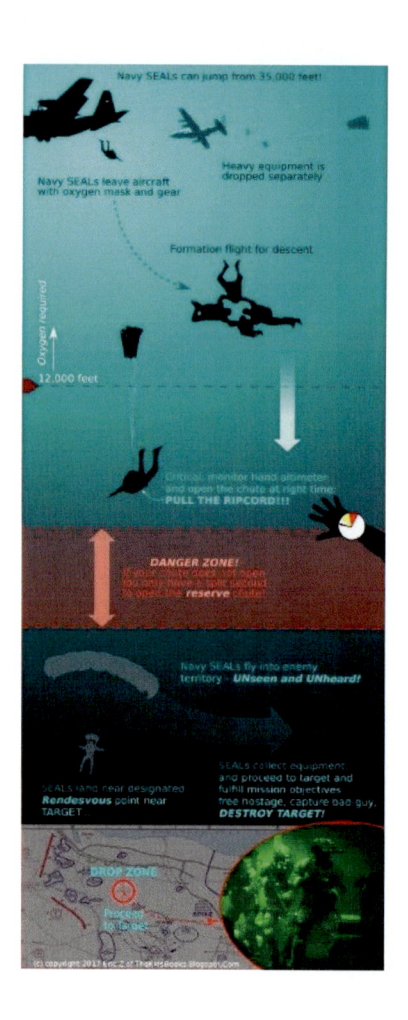

You can get both versions of this high resolution infographic for FREE at thekidsbooks.blogspot.com!

Just type this in any browser:

▸▸bit.ly/navyinfo◂◂

Target

The enemy STRONGHOLD, a fortified house, deep in the jungle where the bad guys are holding the hostage.

The SEALs silently approach the house, from a safe distance...

...their sniper takes out the enemy sentry...

His rifle is fitted with a silencer...*stealth!*

...then the SEALs spring into action ...

The house is BREACHED, the SEALS enter and take out the enemy combatants one by one...

If all is done well, the hostage is not injured during the rescue and the SEALs leave for home...the rendezvous point 5km down river!

Extraction

The team has encountered problems!

One of the bad guys has sounded the alarm...

They will need a HOT EXTRACT fast, *really fast and...*

...HOT means the guns are blazing as they go in—engage the enemy—and WIN!

"Wolfpack--this is Witchdoctor-- requesting immediate HOT EXTRACT-- taking in heavy enemy fire from my 3 O'clock position..."

The Team Leader calls in the HOT EXTRACT

Here they come!

Comin' in Hot Hot Hot!

US NAVY

See a video of a HOT EXTRACT here:
▶▶**bit.ly/hotextract**◀◀

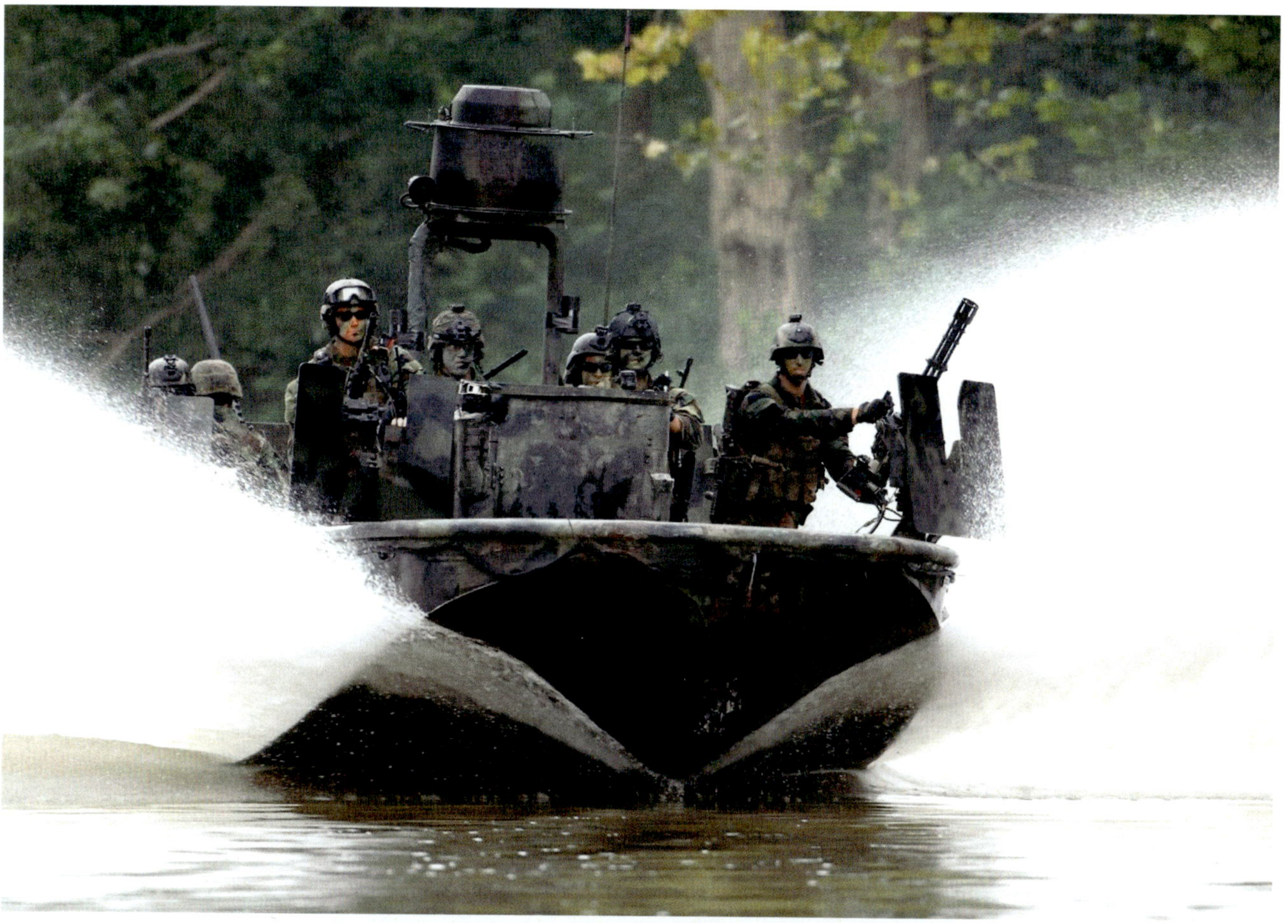

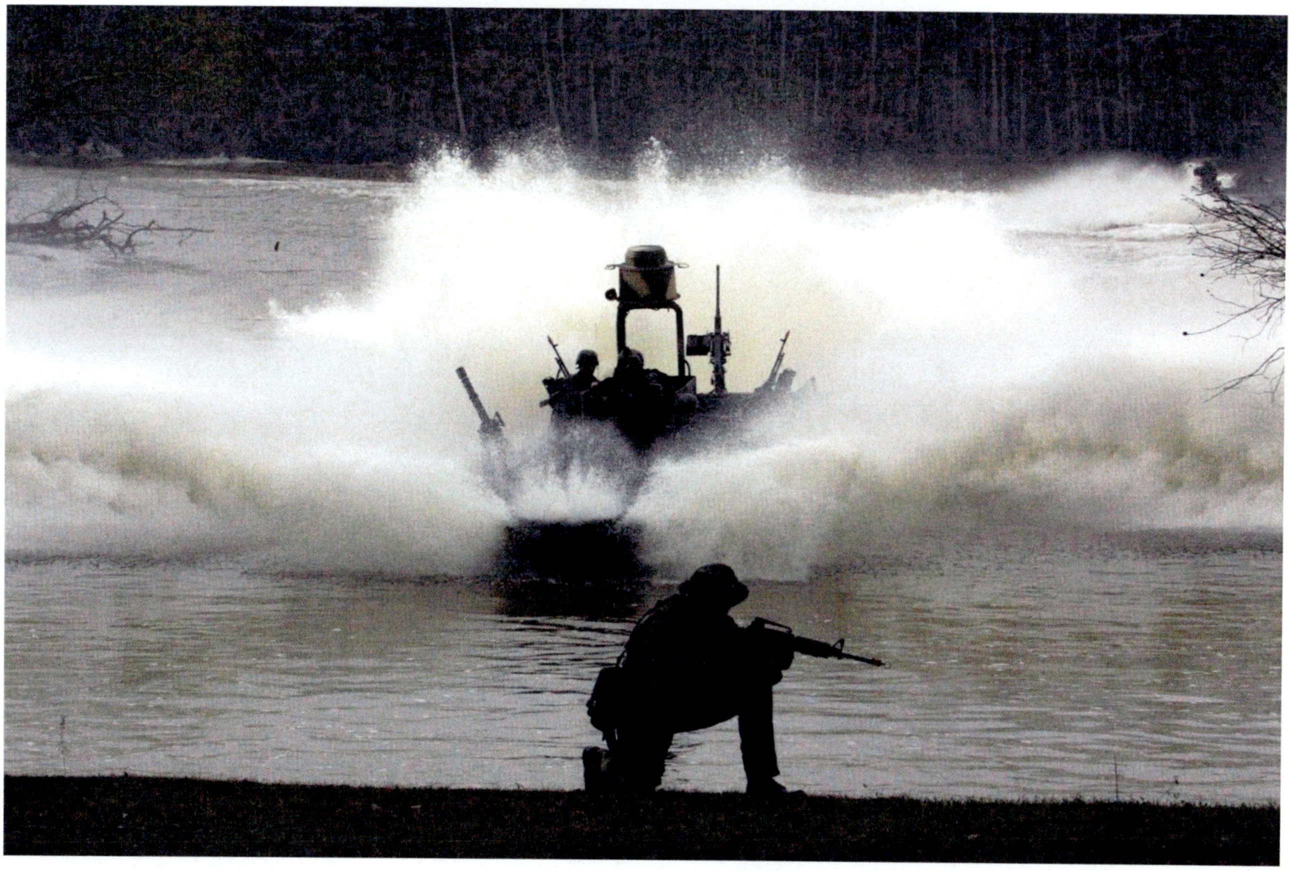

Just in time!

The Minigun spews out six-thousands bullets per minute!

No matter which way the boat turns, there is a gun to lay down COVER FIRE!

The .50 Calibre is smoking!

The special boat teams proceed to "light up" the enemy stronghold...

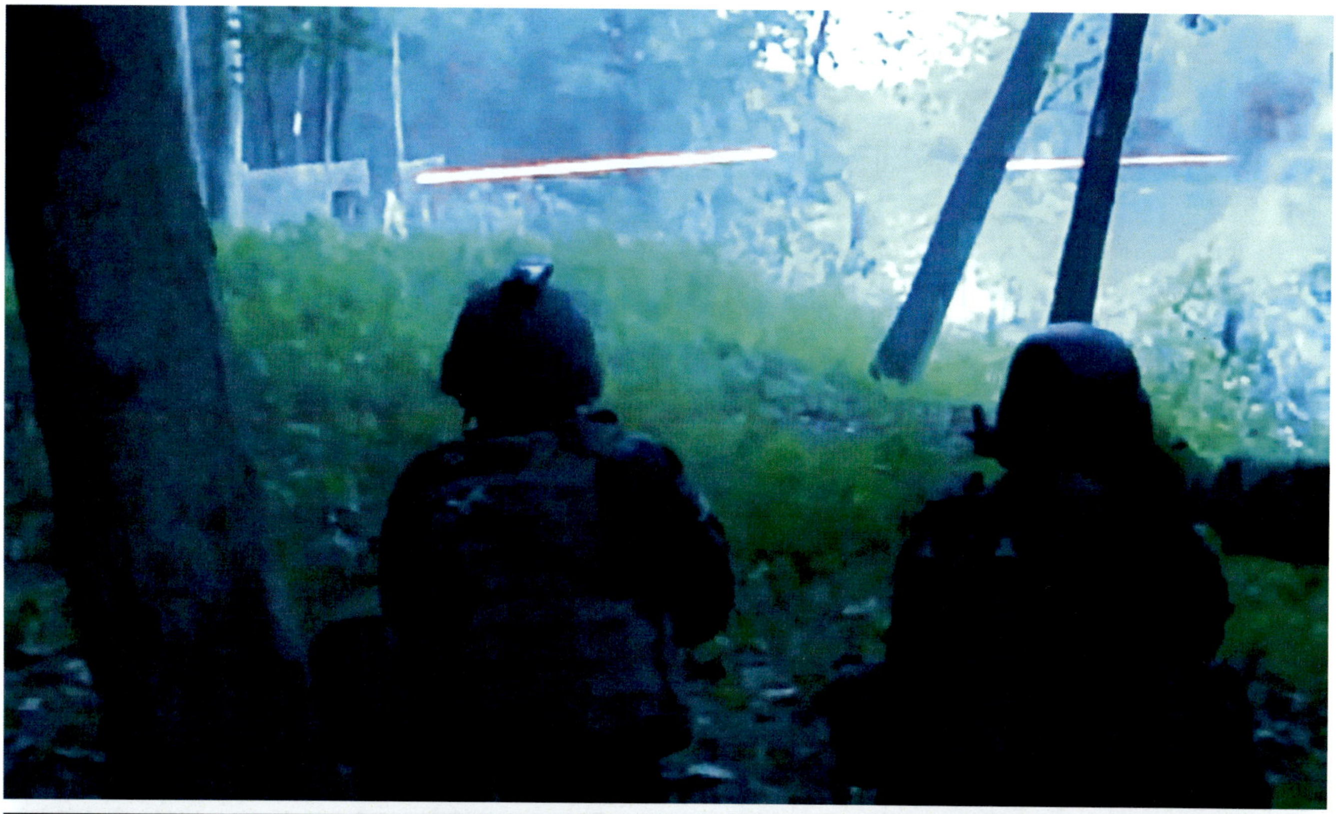

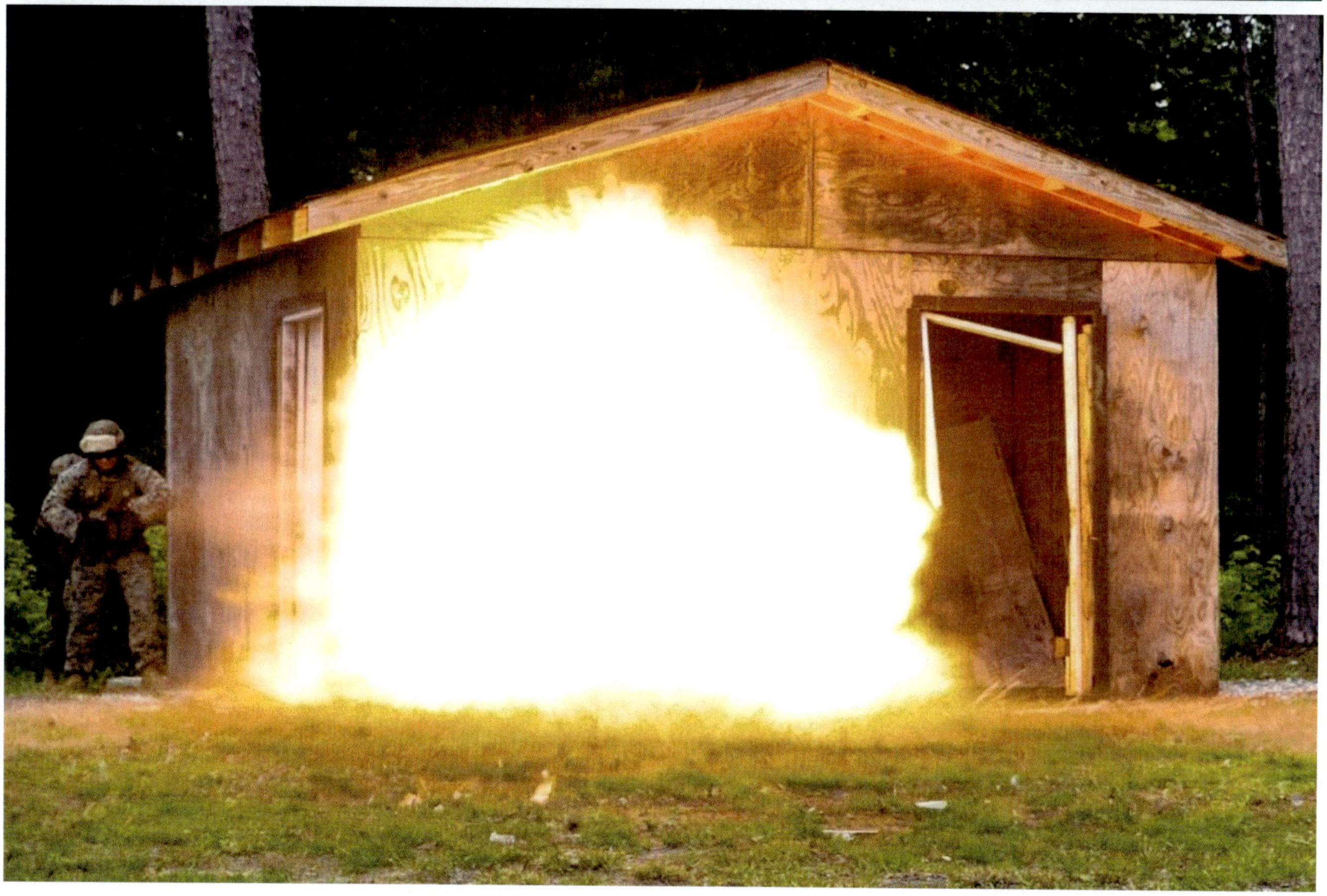

After they OBLITERATE the enemy stronghold, they gather up the team and head for home...

Job well done!

Bonus Section

The U.S. Navy Parachute Team, The Leap Frogs!

For the Leapfrogs schedule go to leapfrogs.navy

136

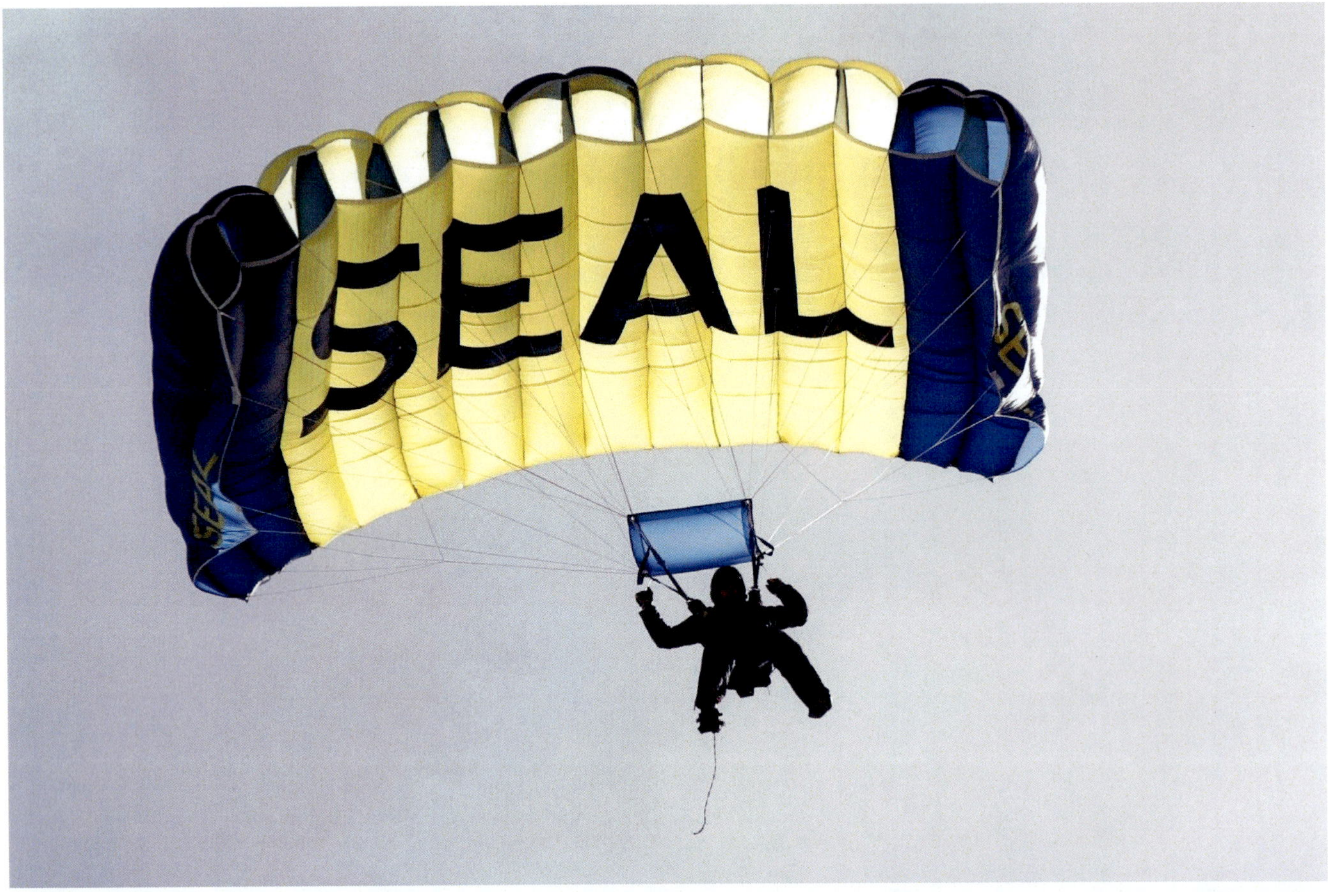
SEAL

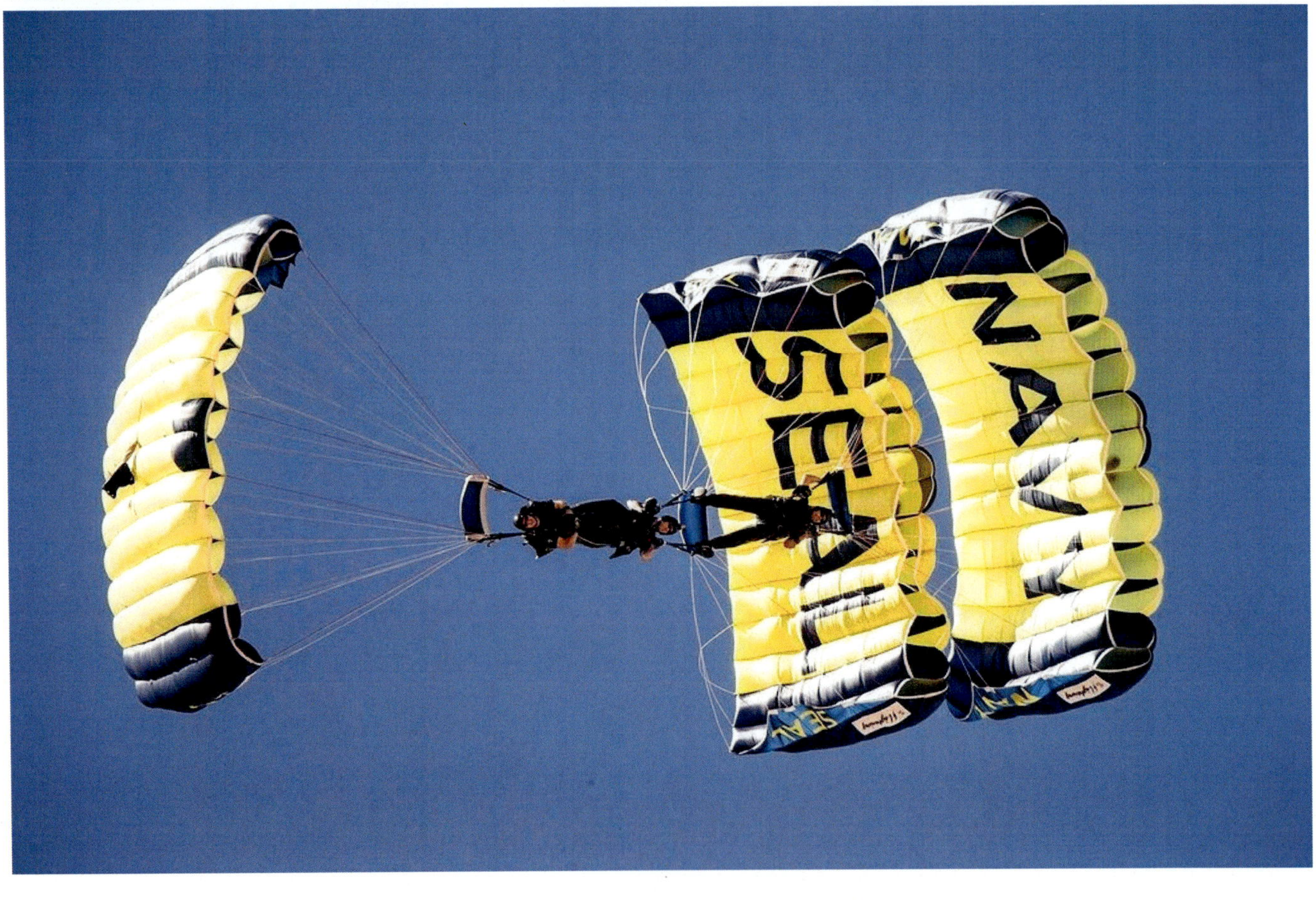
SEAL
NAVY

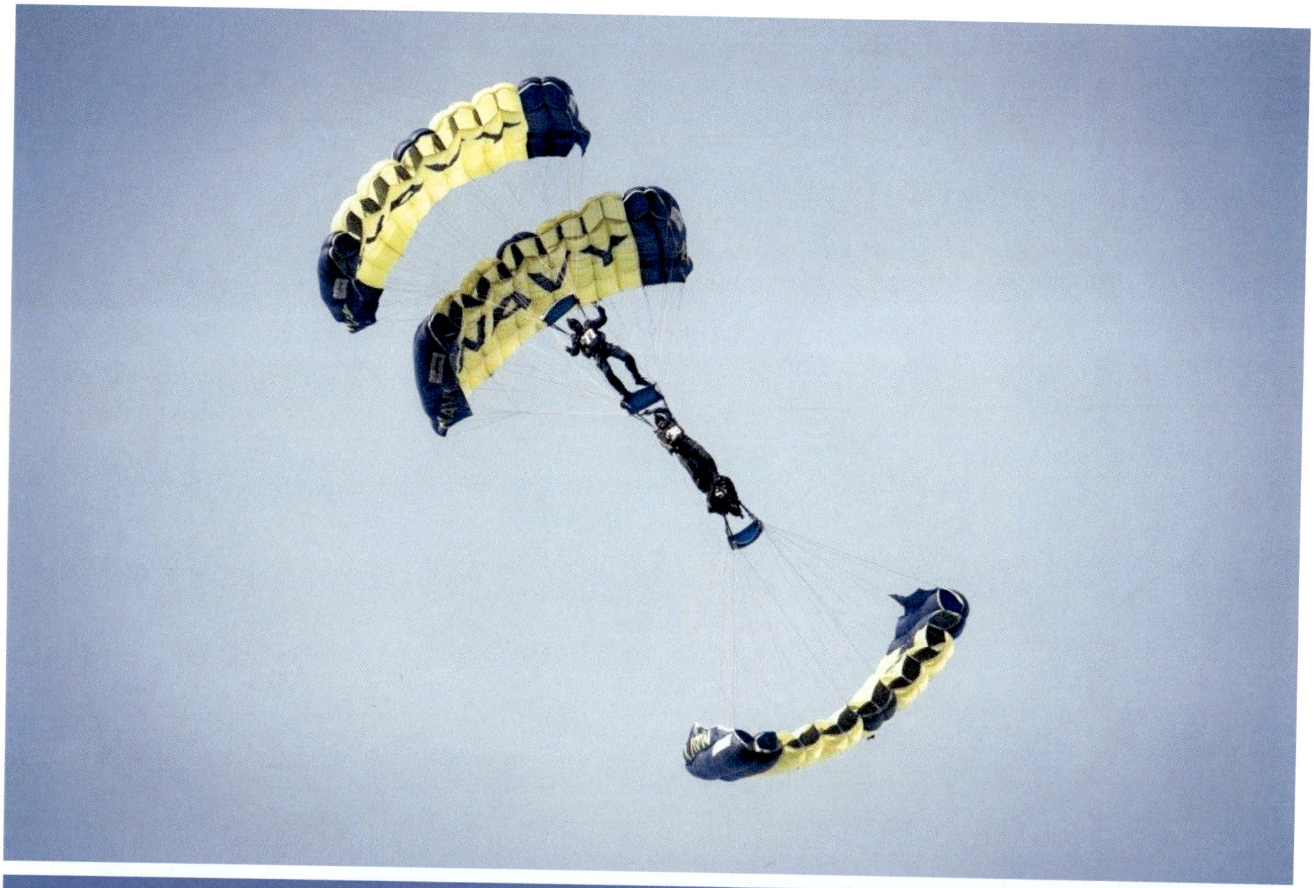
NAVY

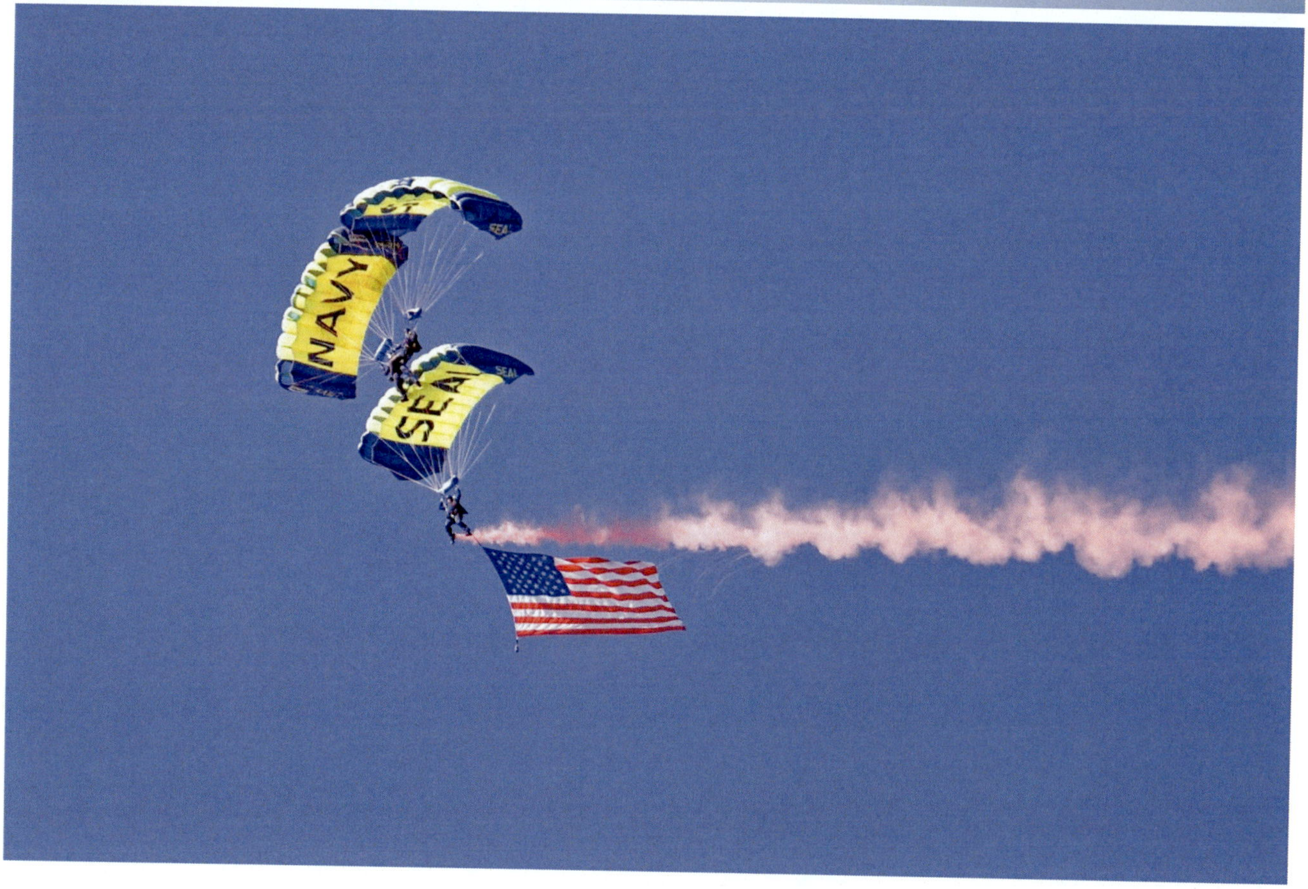
NAVY
SEAL

Tandem coupling is a faster way to descend. They call this "bleeding off altitude."

It also looks cool with smoke pots attached to your feet!

A solo spiral with smoke...

The Navy SEALs Leap Frogs are not just a parachute jump team; they are real Navy SEALs ready to enter combat at anytime and anyplace!

Me too! Just as long as it is near the water!

A tandem spiral trailing multiple smoke pots, can you think of anything funner than that?!

THE END

Your adventure continues here!

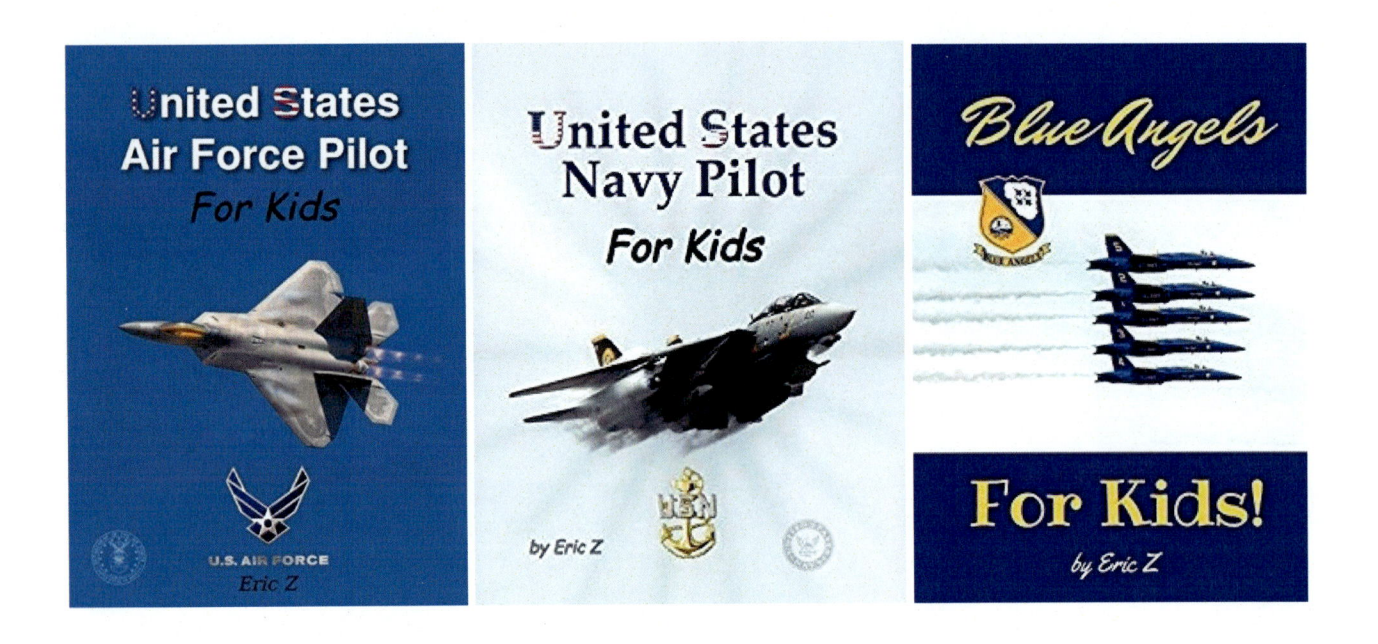

Go to ▶▶**bit.ly/previewz**◀◀

And start your next mission!

Please **HIT SOME STARS** for the **Navy SEALS!**
Go and RATE this book on Amazon!

Go to www.amazon.com/author/ericz